CHEERS, GEOFF!

CHEERS, GEOFF!

TALES FROM THE TOUCHLINE

GEOFF SHREEVES

MACMILLAN

First published 2022 by Macmillan
an imprint of Pan Macmillan
The Smithson, 6 Briset Street, London EC1M 5NR
EU representative: Macmillan Publishers Ireland Ltd, 1st Floor,
The Liffey Trust Centre, 117–126 Sheriff Street Upper,
Dublin 1, D01 YC43
Associated companies throughout the world
www.panmacmillan.com

ISBN 978-1-0350-0639-7

Typeset in Fairfield LT Std by Palimpsest Book Production Ltd, Falkirk, Stirlingshire
Printed and bound by CPI Group (UK) Ltd, Croydon, CR0 4YY

Contents

*'Football is the most important
of the least important things in life.'*
Arrigo Sacchi

For Di, Ellie, Jack and Lottie.
My favourite team.

Foreword

I first met Geoff way back, when I was still playing for Southampton and before the Premier League had even started. He and Sky took a punt that I might have a fairly decent career in front of me and decided to get me on one of their shows. To be fair, I can't really remember it, it was that long ago.

What I do remember is that Shreevesie stayed in touch, and he became one of the people in the media that I grew to trust implicitly – and that's the secret of both his success and his longevity.

For thirty-odd years, he's been a constant presence, either in the tunnel or on the side of the pitch, sticking a microphone under the noses of players and managers, getting that instant reaction.

The fact is, he wouldn't have lasted two minutes if he wasn't good at his job (which he is) and if people in the game didn't trust him. You know he's not going to turn you over or stitch you up because, if he did, the word would have got around in the game, and nobody would give him the time of day. Other television reporters have come and gone but Geoff has been a permanent fixture, content just to do his job superbly.

You know he's going to ask you the tough questions but he does it with an honesty and integrity that isn't looking for the massive headline, he's simply asking the kind of questions that fans and viewers want answered, it's as straightforward as that.

That level of trust and honesty goes a long way in football and it's why I consider him a friend, because he's never let me down and he's never looked to exploit our relationship. We're simply mates, chatting about football and life.

I know that whenever I'm on *Match of the Day* and I've analysed a player or a game, invariably there will be a message from Geoff when I come off air saying, 'That was a decent point,' or, more usually, 'What the fuck were you talking about?'

Over the years, he's been on hand for advice, for help and for the kind of guidance that comes from decades of experience in television. I know I'm not the only player or manager he's helped out over the years, and he does it because he genuinely wants to see people succeed, nothing more than that.

Trust is an invaluable commodity but it's the principle on which Geoff has built his career and it's why he's been so successful. Also, he tells a really good story and this book is packed with them.

CHEERS, GEOFF!

Anyway, that's enough blowing smoke up his backside otherwise he'll think I've gone soft in my old age.

Cheers, Geoff.

Alan Shearer

Prologue

It started, as most life-changing events do, innocuously. I got a call from EA Sports asking me if I would like to be the voice of the pitchside reporter for their FIFA game franchise. Nothing arduous, just half a day's voice recording in a discreet little art deco studio in Soho, me in the sound booth and two engineers on a mixing desk running through a whole range of potential scenarios from groin strains, hamstring tweaks, and twisted ankles, to tactical swaps and the sort of cover-all observations that were part and parcel of any Sky *Super Sunday* interjection from beside the dugouts.

In truth, I didn't know much about the game itself. I thought it was mainly for kids or those in their early twenties who hadn't quite kicked their teenage hobbies. But I was aware of how popular it was and there was a kudos attached to being involved.

This was 2007 and Sky had established themselves as the major player in football broadcasting. Fifteen years after the start of the Premier League and Sky was the byword for state-of-the-art coverage, the best analysis and a drive for the kind of standards few around the world could match. And I was proud of the fact I'd been there from day one, alongside a small band of people who'd been tasked with revolutionizing the way television fans consumed the game. Frankly, at that stage, Sky was untouchable.

So, the FIFA gig was a handy distraction, a break from gunning up and down England's motorway network or flying out to Europe for Sky's Champions League coverage almost every other week. It also helped that Sky's lead commentator, Martin Tyler, was doing a lot of the heavy lifting with the commentary on the FIFA matches, while another great friend, Alan Smith, was the pundit alongside Martin. The three of us were part of a tight-knit Sky team, so this was a bit of a busman's – a few days away from the grind but still doing the job we all loved.

Not that I saw either of them, as they'd recorded their parts in different studios on different days. Basically, Martin's commentary on a fictitious match would be simply driven by the whims and tactics of a gamer and, every now and again, when an incident demanded, he would throw to me, down on the virtual sidelines. My pre-records would fit in with whatever injury or tactical shift the game threw up and my 'character' would then hand back to Martin. His response, every time, would be a swift, 'Cheers, Geoff.'

Cheers, Geoff. Two words. A mere two syllables. But they would come to largely define me for the next fifteen years. Forget all the big-name interviews, the magnificent drama of the Premier League, the World Cups and Champions League finals, I am now as well known for a catchphrase from a computer game as I am for doing my day job for thirty years, despite not actually having ever said it myself.

Mind you, FIFA is not exactly any old computer game, more a global phenomenon. Sitting down to write this book, I quickly googled it and the numbers are astonishing. My musings on groins and hamstrings, substitutions and virtual pitchside observations have been heard by the more than 300 million people who've bought the game over the years, and 'Cheers, Geoff' has actually entered the Urban Dictionary, defined as 'a method of marking the moment when a person makes an unwanted or otherwise unnecessary remark which adds nothing to the conversation or is completely unrelated.'

Thanks, Martin!

There were a few other phrases that resonated with gamers. Even now I still get sent images of gruesome injuries, gunshot wounds or car crashes with the message, 'He's picked up a bad injury but he's a tough cookie and I think he'll be able to carry on' – another go-to line.

But it's 'Cheers, Geoff' that truly resonated. Now it's got its own Facebook page, people have made T-shirts with it emblazoned across the front, while somebody with far more time on their hands than is healthy calculated that 25 per cent of the replies to my posts on Twitter merely consisted of those two words. Fifteen years later, it's a rare day when people don't shout it to me in the street or when I'm in football grounds up and down the country. I was even sent a photograph of somebody who had it tattooed on their backside!

The players got in on the act, too. I'd notice the sneaky little grins as I was interviewing them post-game and about to hand over their Man-of-the-Match award. I'd pass over the champagne, statuette or whatever, and there'd be a little moment's beat before, 'Cheers, Geoff', and they'd be scurrying off back to their dressing room, giggling away like schoolkids who had got one over on a supply teacher.

Up until this point, I had been gently mocked by friends and colleagues for another phrase that Sir Alex Ferguson had coined. His last words to me after virtually every interview — and there were probably thousands over the years — seemed to be always 'Well done, Geoff', as if I had just passed a test. Which, in a way, was fitting, because dealing with Fergie was always an examination of your credibility as a reporter in his eyes. More on Sir Alex later.

I love the fact 'Cheers, Geoff' has become something of a signature because it wasn't planned, it took on a life of its own and it's always said with a smile. It's also part of what has been the most memorable three decades of my life and career, a career that has taken me to every continent, to the very heart of football, where I've met the most inspiring characters and made the truest of friends. It's not always been easy or straightforward, there have been times when my physical and mental health have suffered, when I feared my career was over before it had barely begun, and when I've made mistakes which still leave a chill hand on my spine when I recall them.

But looking back over these last thirty years, I know it's been a privilege from start to . . . well, I won't say finish, because there are still many touchlines to tread, tunnels to stalk and people to interview.

It's been my good fortune to work alongside so many talented and wise people and it's always the words of my father, John, that ring true to me when he said if you do a job you love, you'll never work a day in your life. I'll drink to that.

Cheers, Dad.

1

All Roads DO Lead to Rome

I'm certainly not the first person in life to have had no idea what career they wanted. Neither am I the first person to have had an utterly unexpected change of career. But when I look back at the teenage me, I can see how the four passions I had – football, music, people and, rather improbably, buildings – shaped my life.

Football and music are standards for many teenage boys and girls. And, as far as people are concerned, I've always been comfortable in different company and can readily adapt to any situation, chatting and listening, hear them tell their stories.

As for buildings, well, they were always a fascination that I initially thought would determine my whole career. I could not have been more wrong.

There was absolutely no hardship to my early life, just a gloriously unencumbered upbringing in St Albans with

Mum and Dad, Jean and John – and my two brothers, Graham and Jonathan with me in the middle. Football dominated; *Match of the Day* if we were allowed to stay up on Saturday nights, *The Big Match* on Sunday, and then straight into the garden to replay the action we'd just seen.

I was an enthusiastic footballer, an enthusiasm sadly not matched by ability. I was, to quote the immortal words of Joe Royle, slower than a weekend in prison, but I've always loved playing. School, Cubs, local Sunday team; then, when I was older, training in the week and playing with my mates on the local Astroturf pitch on a Tuesday night. Wonderful stuff.

School came a long way second to football. I was very sociable and very talkative but wasn't exactly setting the world alight academically. I was the only boy in my year that didn't get a letter suggesting next steps, what A levels might be attainable and an outline of a potential career path. When I went to see my head of year and told him I had no letter, he simply replied, 'That's because we have no doubts you won't be here next year because you won't pass any O levels.' Disappointing, but he was nearly right. I left school with a solitary English language O level.

Another one of my dad's sayings is that a good education's key to making balanced decisions, so he was pleased when I told him I had decided to try the local College of Further Education to re-sit six exams. Mind you, I had ulterior motives, given that I'd been to an all-boys' school and the college was mixed, so any prospect of adding to my less than lengthy list of qualifications was actually not my first priority.

My parents still laugh about my college end-of-term

report, which arrived after ten months of supposed 'knuck-ling down', not just taking education seriously but crucially building a platform for a career. Two comments in particular stand out. One tutor remarked, 'I understand Geoff to be an extremely popular, sociable young man. Having never met him, I cannot comment.' Another one just wrote, 'Who?' While there was no hope that I'd suddenly discover a previously well-hidden academic prowess (I did manage to double my previous tally of a solitary O level by passing GCE English literature too), I did meet my future wife, Di, although it was a good few years before we actually started going out. Time well spent on that basis, in my book.

Suddenly the realization hit that I was coming up for eighteen years old and didn't really have any idea of a career. One thing that interested me was buildings and, specifically, houses. My dad built up a hugely successful quantity surveying practice and was involved in the construction of large-scale commercial property, but for me it was houses. I used to devour the local and national property press, looking at different styles, learning what I liked and didn't like in terms of architecture, interior design – the details fascinated me. I really don't know where this interest came from, but it has stayed with me. Later on in life I would buy and sell, renovate, design and build homes, including the one we live in to this day. Back then it was purely just an interest of mine but enough of one to trigger my next course of action.

I decided to write to the six or seven estate agents in St Albans, and stuck a letter through the door of each of them, asking if they had any jobs going. I got one reply, from a company called Allwright & Partners, run by Nick Allwright – a beer-drinking, rally-car-driving, macho rugby type – and Nic Savage, who was a former male model; a suave, happily married guy, who embraced the arts and culture. Polar opposites as people, but good guys to learn from.

The business was nothing like the highly functioning digitized, slick operations they all are now. We employed a secretary, Diana, to whom you could dictate letters, and Mavis, who was the office manager and a highly skilled printer in charge of this huge, Caxton-type printing press in the back office. Once we'd put a house on the market, she'd be in there churning out details sheets with the place covered in black ink. No colour and certainly no photocopier. When people from out of town came in enquiring about the area, I would give them a map and draw on it a dotted line where the M25 was to be built. Allwright & Partners certainly wasn't antiquated, far from it, Nick and Nic were forward-thinking, ambitious guys, it was just of its time. It was also a great way to start for a kid with no experience.

It was an incredible window into people's worlds. After death or divorce, you are entrusted with placing a financial appraisal on probably the most valuable asset they'll probably ever own. In time you become adept at this but, in the early days, I had to leave myself plenty of wriggle room just in case the figure I announced was not the one they were expecting.

Obviously, you'd do your homework beforehand, but when you hit them with a price and they say, open-mouthed, 'As much as that?' I would then hastily add, 'Well, you know, if you've got a long time to sell it, if you've got time on your hands and you're not in a particular hurry, blah, blah, blah – but obviously a more realistic price might be this.' And then you'd talk it down a bit.

But if they said, 'Is that all?' then you'd tell them that was the price only if they had to leave the country the next day, and that such a ridiculously low price was only there to attract the quickest of sales . . . tap-dancing all the way.

Then you had to take a photo of the house to put in the local paper. No mobile phones, so we had to use what they called a 'land camera', which was very similar to a black-and-white Polaroid. Once you had taken the snap you had to wait for five minutes while the picture materialized. I used to place the very expensive camera on the roof of my car while I waited, but unfortunately developed a habit where, once satisfied with the snap, I would drive off, completely forgetting about the camera!

I got to meet some real characters. John Gordon ran a local garage where we would take our company cars to be serviced. I liked him enormously because he was such a gruff, grizzled old chap who took no BS from anyone. For whatever reason his house was proving particularly difficult to sell. All the agents in town had tried and failed, so I just pestered him to let me have a go. For some reason, he always called me Godfrey, never Geoff, but eventually I wore him down and he gave me a shot.

I worked night and day on it and eventually found somebody who wanted it, agreed a price and we exchanged contracts. Chuffed with myself, I went down to John's garage, where I found him working on a car, covered in grease and oil as usual. Tapping him on the shoulder, I told him I'd sold his house as promised. I'm not sure what I expected, perhaps a 'That's fantastic news,' or, 'Well done, Godfrey.' Instead, he looked me square in the eye and – without betraying a single emotion – simply uttered the words I'll never forget, 'Well, swallow me knob!'

There has always been a side of me that likes to develop things, whether it's a property, an idea for TV, a book, anything. Once I get my teeth into it, I need to not only see it through to the end, but also make it the best it can possibly be, and apply creativity to the process. It was like that with the estate agency. I wanted to do more with the business so, when one of the partners left, I bought into the partnership around the time things were going well and we were opening satellite offices around the area in local towns and villages.

This was in the mid-Eighties when, if you didn't mind working hard, you could build yourself a decent career. I had been fortunate enough to buy my first house when I was twenty-one and, for six or seven years, I'd grafted to build the business and create something for myself in terms of livelihood. A lot of people think that because I'm a good talker is why I was a successful estate agent. It's partially true, but the main reason was because I was – and am – a good listener. So often exasperated couples would sit in front of me, with reams of details from other agents all totally unsuited to their requirements, and it would be down to me to explain exactly what they needed or wanted.

With St Albans being so close to Arsenal's training ground at London Colney in Hertfordshire, it was inevitable we would cross paths with footballers. The first player I met was Alan Smith, who signed for Arsenal for

£850,000 in March 1987, but was loaned back to Leicester City for the rest of that season until moving down permanently in the summer. Alan, who is known to everyone as 'Smudge', came into the offices with his future wife, Penny, on the hunt for a place within striking distance of both the training ground and Highbury. So, I showed more interest than usual because I was a football fan and, rather than just give them some photocopies, I went the extra mile and offered to take them around, show them the area and do everything I could to help them out. Frankly, they were terrible clients; twice I've sold them houses, twice they've asked for rural locations, older houses with beams, quirky, with character, and twice they've bought brand new houses! Mind you, it's thirty-five years since we met and we're still great friends, so they must have been happy with the service . . .

Football is a very insular world, and whether it's houses, cars, clothes, financial advice, whatever, it's, 'Who's the guy we need to see? Who do we go to?' So off the back of selling Smudge his house, he asked me to look after this young lad called Lee Dixon who Arsenal had signed from Stoke City. He was living in a hotel, with his family back up north and, frankly, he was bored, so Smudge asked if I would take him out for a pizza and a beer.

With the business flying, I enjoyed the trappings of success with a soft-top sports car with a phone in it and a house of my own at a relatively young age. So, I took Lee out and we got chatting, we're getting on well with each other when he asked if he could use my phone? Not a problem.

He called his wife and said, 'I'm with this lad, I'm in

his car, he's got a phone in his car, he's got his own house and he's got his own business – he's fucking Billy Big Time!' He christened me Billy and, to this day, there's a certain group of people who still call me Billy.

From there followed Steve Bould, again coming down from Stoke, and Brian Marwood, who I helped find a house. Through Smudge, I got invited to go to Arsenal a lot. Paul Merson, Nigel Winterburn and Kevin Richardson all lived in the area too. In fact, St Albans was often the starting point for their famous Tuesday drinking club. It was fantastic fun, seeing this team come together under George Graham – all young, all hungry; not millionaires, just a group of determined lads with something to prove.

About that time, however, I started to get disillusioned with what I call the small-town mentality. Having grown up in St Albans, gone to school and college and (vaguely) played football there, drunk in the pubs, I thought there had to be more to life than that, I had to expand my horizons. So I sold my shares in the business and decided to get into property development as opposed to just selling houses.

At this point in the Eighties, property prices were still booming and footballers were interested in buying houses or land and having somebody develop them. It was a buoyant, bustling scene and I was in the middle of it. I ran the New York marathon for fun, and to raise cash for a local charity, went on nice holidays. Life was good.

Well, until it wasn't.

When I tell people that I lost every single penny I had and they ask me how, the explanation is very simple to demonstrate. Hold your left hand about four feet above the ground: everything under it was the cost of acquiring the land or properties, the cost of owning it, servicing the interest on the debt, legal fees, everything – that was my outlay, that is what it cost. Now put your right hand a foot above your left which marks what it was worth. Everything between belonged to me and was my profit.

In the late Eighties, I was in the middle of a perfect storm of a property crash and an interest rate spike that went from around 3 per cent to about 16 per cent in what felt like a week. That's when your right hand sinks a foot below your left and you are left with plummeting values, spiralling costs and a whole mountain of debt. Your hands may have changed place but what is between them still belongs to you.

I thought I was gone, over. I avoided bankruptcy but filed for voluntary liquidation, but everything went: my confidence, my ego, my pride; they all went out the window alongside my bank balance. Those same banks that have been slow to lend are pretty quick to call in their loans. My house was mortgaged to the hilt, I had nothing to my name, I was in about as desperate a position as anybody can be.

For a long time, I was lost, and I couldn't see any way out. Frankly, I would have done anything to earn a few quid, just as long as I could hold my head up and say I was working my hardest to get out of the hole in which I found myself. And not only myself, because by that time I was with Di.

Across the road from my old office was a family firm of insurance brokers run by two brothers, Kevin and Brian Luckhurst, who I had got to know really well because they insured all our properties at the estate agency. On the wall of their office were pictures of their younger brother, Mick. Now everybody who had gone to the same school as Mick, knew him. He was an incredible athlete; an England under-19 triallist at rugby, he played basketball for Great Britain schools and had a single-figure golf handicap in his teens.

He'd gone to a college that had an American exchange programme because he thought he stood a chance of making it in pro basketball. That wasn't going to happen, but while he was playing rugby out there and taking the conversions, somebody challenged him to try kicking an American football.

Always up for a challenge, Mick asked what the record distance was and, after being told it was sixty-three yards, he marked out the distance and, without even a kicking tee, launched the ball two out of three times between the posts. That won him a college scholarship, from where he went on to the National Football League (NFL) with the Atlanta Falcons. He played for seven years, becoming their leading points-scorer by the time he retired, and then became the face of Channel 4's American football coverage.

Anyway, here I am in early 1990, with no prospects, no land, no job, potless, down on my luck and with no solid prospects on the horizon. So, I decide to pop in and see Kevin because he's always good for a positive word and a pick-me-up. Not unusually, Kev was on the phone, but I have no idea who he's talking to, all I hear is, 'Yeah, yeah, the bloke you need has just walked into my office. All right, cheers,' and he put the phone down.

'Who was that?' I asked.

'My brother, he could have some work for you.'

'Oh great, has Brian got some property that needs sorting out or building work?' I would have taken anything. Labouring, clearing a garden or building a patio would have been a gift from heaven at that point.

'No. That was my brother Mick, he's covering the World Cup in Italy for CNN in the summer and he needs a spotter and I've told him you're the perfect man.'

'Great, brilliant, I appreciate it. Just one question, what the fuck is a spotter?'

It turns out a spotter is someone who watches the game alongside the commentator and co-commentator, known as a 'colour' commentator in the States. The spotter's job is to pick up nuggets of information from a game that the two main guys might have missed. He's also in charge of collating every last scrap of information, statistics and gossip about every single player, manager, referee, linesman, and whoever else the commentators might need to talk about.

So, I asked Kevin where exactly I fitted into this scenario. 'Don't worry,' he replied, 'you'll be perfect for it, you know football.' I did know football, but only to watch it and chat about it with mates. I had no expertise, and I certainly didn't have the foggiest idea where to start in this supposed spotter's role. A little while later, I spoke to Mick, and he told me he was coming over from the States to do a couple of pre-World Cup games that would act as an audition for a few people he thought might be suitable for the role.

That's when blind panic takes over. But by sheer fluke, my mum used to play squash with John Motson's wife Anne, and the next time they got together, she mentioned that I was up for a job and could John, possibly, give me any words of advice?

I will be eternally grateful to John for all his help and time. Here he was, a broadcasting legend, confronted by a potless property developer, asking about a job that doesn't really exist in British television. To say he was somewhere between confused and discombobulated is probably an understatement, yet he was so generous and patient as he showed me how to write out a commentator's board and what to include. Motty's boards are a work of art, a supreme example of the kind of journalism unique to commentators, a couple of which he gave me to take away and learn from. They were worth their weight in gold.

I have so much for which to thank the Luckhurst family, it's impossible to put down in words how much they changed my life; from Kev being the most incredible pal and making the introduction that changed my life beyond recognition, to Mick somehow having faith in me, down to Brian's sons, Tim and Ben, who generously gave me their Panini sticker albums so I could research all the players before I joined Mick for the two games which would be my audition for a new world. It might well have been schoolboy stuff, but I needed all the help I could get.

Mick duly came over and we went to a friendly international in France to do a dummy run. We stood on a gantry where the cameras are mounted and commentators sit. There I was, with Motty-style boards, a copy of *World Soccer* magazine, my Panini sticker book and not much else in the way of preparation, other than a determination to soak up as much information as possible. I have to say,

I was proud of my boards until, just before kick-off, Mick said, 'What can you tell me about the number four?'

'It's all there on the boards,' I replied.

'But what if I lose the boards?' he countered.

'Well, don't lose the fucking boards.'

Hmm, probably not the best move, and I really thought I might be going straight home after that first game. Instead, we put that little glitch behind us and retreated to a bar. This was my first experience of a night out with Mick and to say he's never taken a backward step in his life would be an understatement. There was a rather large Frenchman at the bar, and I had the distinct feeling things could go up a notch or two, but in the end it was all smiles and beers and rugby talk, and we escaped without incident.

For the next game a week later in Holland, not only did I prepare the boards assiduously, I also memorized them as well as making other notes for myself. Basically, I did a top job. Except that both managers decided they wanted to look at so many different players that the squads were completely unrecognizable from the notes I'd prepared. If there were forty players on display, then I've got notes for about six of them. Fair to say, it does not go well.

After the game, I'm licking my wounds, convinced I was straight out of there, never to come close to the World Cup, back to being a skint St Albans property developer. Again, I've got so much to thank Motty for, because the BBC were also doing the game and he invited Mick and me out for a drink. Last hurrah time, I'm drinking and chatting with Motty and the BBC guys, Mick's having a great time and at least it feels like I've gone out on a high, even if it is simply reflected glory from knowing John Motson.

Three days later, I meet Mick at my house and I'm all for shaking his hand, thanking him for the opportunity and wishing him luck at the World Cup because I've got no chance of the gig.

Mick started with those fateful words, 'Can I be brutally honest with you?' – and you know it's going to be downhill from there. He made it clear that the job of the spotter was to make him look good, nothing else. He was the American football star who supported Manchester United and watched games but who needed someone professional to ensure he was never embarrassed by a lack of knowledge or information on air. He had the profile, and he wasn't about to let that be damaged by some bumbling fool.

He then told me he'd interviewed another couple of guys back in the States who were traditional stats men, who were already employed as spotters and who had an ency-clopaedic knowledge of the players, their stories and every pertinent iota of information. They were exactly what he was looking for.

'Geoff, I can't sugar-coat this,' he said. 'The other two guys are what I need. Secondly, I can't describe how poor you've been over those two games.' It's done. The axe has fallen and I can't argue with a word of his condemnation.

'But if you think I'm spending six weeks of my life with two of the most boring people it's been my misfortune to meet in life, then you're very mistaken.'

In a decision verging on insanity, and certainly against his better judgement, to my complete and utter astonish-ment Mick gave me the job. He told me I would get better.

Why, I asked, because there's potential? No, apparently because, in his words, 'You can't get any worse!' He later conceded I'd been unlucky in the second match, that there had been improvement, but I was left under no illusion that I'd got the job neither on talent nor ability.

The USA hadn't qualified for a World Cup in forty years, so there was going to be a huge spotlight on them, not just from the American viewing audience but for their novelty value to the rest of the world. I devoured everything I could get my hands on about them and the other twenty-three teams who would be in Italy: videotapes, cuttings from every newspaper going. I chatted with Smudge about England, and with other journalists who knew Mick from his Falcons exploits, so I tapped into them as much as I could. I was very fortunate that I met the brilliant Keir Radnedge, who worked at World Soccer and was kind enough to help me out with so much information and insight.

One thing that also helped was CNN's budget for the tournament. Even before we'd flown out to Italy, I'd been able to buy a mini-TV with a built-in VHS player, so Mick and I could sit down before every game and watch all the tapes I'd collected. The idea was we would view tapes of each team the night before we covered them. The trunk weighed a ton and cost a fortune in excess baggage. We never even opened it! No matter, both Mick and myself realized this was an incredible opportunity and we were determined not to let it slip through our hands.

We arrived in Rome and drove out to the villa where Mick was staying with the other CNN 'talent', a beautiful place with pool, tennis court, five-a-side pitch. I was staying down the road with the other production staff and was envisaging some hostel where we'd all be grubbing around while the stars lived in the lap of luxury.

Instead, we rocked up at a villa that I can only describe as the most opulent, magnificent country house I have ever seen before or since. It was owned by the composer who scored the film *Amadeus*, and basically you would not have been surprised if it had hot and cold running champagne on tap. It was sumptuous, with its own pool, a fleet of drivers at our disposal and there was nothing you couldn't ask for. If this was working in television, man, I could get used to it.

I wasn't greeted necessarily with open arms by the American production staff, and it was pretty clear there were two main problems. Firstly, I was English and completely inexperienced. Secondly, I was seen as merely Mick's mate and not here on any merit. All that did was forge a deeper bond between Mick and me. We *loved* it, going to so many different matches and all the England games in what was a brilliant tournament for Bobby Robson's team. I'd been transported to a different world, one that I adored. Quite literally, from the moment I arrived I was enthralled and transfixed in equal measure.

To be honest, we were outsiders amongst the English media pack. They were always friendly, but we didn't have any relationship with them and, by and large, it was just Mick and me, driving around Italy, living high on CNN's dollar. Mick's favourite tipple was Dom Pérignon and even now, when we've had a bit too much of the bubbly, it's still known as brain domage, something that has stuck for three decades.

One day, we were stood at the bar alone, chatting with our backs to the room when we heard someone say, 'Excuse me, I'm sorry to bother you, but are you Mick Luckhurst?' We both turned around, eager to meet a friendly face, then both our jaws hit the floor. Standing in front of us was Sir Bobby Charlton, Mick's boyhood hero and a player he had worshipped growing up. In fact, Mick's middle name is Robert in honour of Sir Bobby. It transpired that Bobby was a huge American football fan and watched Mick on Channel 4 each week.

Later in the tournament, on the night England were knocked out in the semi-finals, we bumped into Sir Bobby outside the stadium. Mick would have loved to have picked up where we had left off in the bar previously, but defeat had hit Sir Bobby particularly hard and it was clear this proud Englishman was in no mood for idle chat.

It was a fantastic, kaleidoscopic adventure for me, a wonderful introduction to international travel and just football, football, football. It didn't take me long after stepping into this alien world that I decided that it was where I wanted my future to lie. This was a wonderful dream-like existence that I was determined to make my life. I might have known the square root of zero about television, football and journalism, but all three subjects fascinated me and the thought of being able to earn a living from the combination of all three was simply mind-blowing. But how? was the big question. Contacts – I decided very early on – was the key to prolonging this. I soaked up as much knowledge as possible and made a conscious decision to network as ferociously as I could in order to capitalize on the opportunity I'd been given.

One of my earliest contacts, which turned into a thirty-year plus friendship, started at one of the broadcast centres. I was photocopying some notes and statistics when I got talking to Martin Tyler, who was working for the nascent BSkyB even in those days. I obviously recognized him and struck up conversation.

Anyway, we got chatting and it became very clear that while Martin might have had a cursory interest in this young fellow from England, it wasn't my patter or youthful appearance that made an impact, rather the reams of expensively produced and collated stats I had under my arm! We agreed to stay in touch when we got home and, it has to be said, Martin has been an influential ever present in my broadcasting career.

The whole experience was a massive education condensed into a month. Frankly, I wasn't much help to the American production team because I was more Mick's personal assistant. But I did learn about being a runner. Going back and forth between the tunnel area, picking up information, bringing it back to the gantry or the production centre, learning my way around stadia, discovering what went on behind the scenes of putting on a television broadcast.

There were also moments that the viewers never see or realize what is happening behind the scenes. We were covering West Germany versus Holland in the first knockout stage in Milan's San Siro and while most people will remember it for Frank Rijkaard spitting at Rudi Völler and both men getting sent off, I recall it for another confrontation between Mick and a Frenchman.

Mick was trying to squeeze past the French commentary

team to get to his seat in the press box but one of the French crew wasn't making it easy. In fact, he was being downright obstructive and belligerent. Tempers were fraying, voices were raised, insults were thrown, and this rather large French unit was on his feet and making it clear there was only one way to settle things. All this while we were on air.

CNN co-commentator, Bob Neil, was not the funniest of men but he took his headphones off, pointed at the combative Frenchman and said, 'Hey, to save time, why don't you go outside and practise falling down and bleeding. Then I'll send him out in ten minutes.' It was a brilliant line and, after it had been translated, completely defused the situation and we ended up having drinks and a laugh after the game together.

I did eventually prove myself as a spotter doing exactly what I was supposed to do when England were locked at 0-0 with Holland and Stuart Pearce smashes in a free kick. Up goes Mick, off on one 'England have done it!! What a brilliant goal from the left back.' I, however, have spotted that the ref has disallowed it as it was an indirect free kick but Mick is having none of it. 'That's England, Fight to the end, never give up and you will win,' while I'm desperately tugging at his sleeve, in fact, hanging off him. Game ends, 0-0, few words from Bob and we go off air with the viewers thinking England won. Mick turns and says, 'That was sensational, what did you want to say to me?'

So many astonishing memories, like being in the television booth next to the BBC radio commentary team and hearing the great Bryon Butler in full flow and being mesmerized at his brilliance with words and beautifully rich voice. Or making up for missing my brother Graham's wedding by filming what should have been my best man's speech with a proper cameraman and Mick chipping in with best wishes to the bride and groom. Or sitting in the best hotel in Florence, at a writing desk with the window wide open, feeling like Lord Byron. When I look back, I still cannot comprehend how lucky I was for those four brilliant weeks at having stepped into a different world.

The money helped, too. I picked up one of the most vital of all journalism tips during the tournament, how to manipulate the world of expense! At first, Mick and I were circumspect about claiming for meals and drinks, we weren't kicking the arse out of it by any means.

But by the end of the trip, we could have claimed we were buying a meal for Walter Winterbottom and nobody back in the States would have blinked an eye, they simply signed it off.

CNN were incredibly generous, and at the end of the tournament I got paid a handsome amount. Not enough to completely dig myself out of the financial hole I'd been in before the World Cup, but it went some way to helping.

The problem was, I was desperate for this experience not to be a one-off. I'd been bitten by the bug; television was all that I now wanted to do. It was an ache, a hunger for this life to continue and for me to be able to carve a career in television football. I naively thought Italia '90 would put me on the map with all the networks, but I was back to square one with just a month's experience under my belt.

I would have done anything just to keep mine and Di's head above water. The knock-on from the property crash and my business going belly up was that we were skint for quite a few years to come, so much so that it was only the generosity of good friends like Smudge and Penny that kept us going.

The four of us had been invited to Penny's brother Greg's wedding in Devon, but Di and I had to decline because we couldn't afford a hotel room for an overnight stay and it was madness to think we could drive to Devon and back in a day. Smudge wouldn't hear of it. There were no rooms left in the hotel so he simply invited us to share their room, getting an extra bed put in. I remember it vividly because we all woke up the next morning, possibly a little worse for wear, and he got up and went out to a car from the FA that was taking him to meet up with England ahead of Euro '92.

So, I did a bit of everything, including overseeing the opening of a pal's wine bar in Harpenden for a while called, fittingly, Billy's. I've still got the original sign for it at home, a fella with a champagne glass in one hand and a cigar in the other. Not sure where they got the inspiration for it . . .

What did I know about running a bar? Zero, except that even your best friends are no longer your best friends when they've had a good drink and that food and booze somehow mysteriously walks out of the door unless it's nailed down, nicked before you could even blink.

But Di and I muddled through. I had been in pubs most of my life, I got on with people and I was organized, I knew who was taking liberties and who could be trusted. It was the sort of place that I would have wanted to frequent if I was a punter, and I treated people the way I would like to have been treated if I was paying. Di is a great cook, so oversaw the menus, the chef and the kitchen and we got down to business as a strong partnership.

I roped in my younger brother, Jonathan, when he was back from university at Christmas, the thinking being that he'd probably spent more time in bars than lectures. He asked who the staff were, only to be told to look in the mirror and he'd find out.

It was a real battle to be open on time, but we scraped in under the wire, even if a few people got wet paint on their clothes from walls that were still drying. We couldn't afford any art or photos for the walls, so I asked an old school friend Andrew Wilson who was a picture framer if he could help out. He went out and bought some picture frames then put some paper down on the floor, dipped his feet and hands in different coloured paint and walked over the paper before framing the results. Let's just say the reaction from the patrons was mixed, although I do know we sold a couple.

My trusty Gunners friends, Smudge, Lee and Bouldy kindly opened Billy's for us and Mick Harford, who lived in Harpenden, was a regular. Unsurprisingly, we didn't have a moment's trouble when people learned it was Mick's local. He is a smashing guy and was nothing but a well ordered and loyal customer as well as being a hugely underrated player given he won two England caps, but his mere presence and reputation as one of football's more ferocious characters probably kept any potential aggro well away from us. Cheers, Mick.

A few things began to turn my way. I got introduced via Mick Luckhurst to a guy called Mike Wilmot who was a match director for a company called Double Bill, who used to produce and televise a First Division game each weekend (this was a few years before the start of the Premier League).

Mike's company looked after the foreign commentators who were at the game, providing all the facilities and logistics they needed for the match, and he employed me as a man on the ground, feeding back all the relevant information, getting the teams from the ref before the game and liaising from inside the stadium, while he sat in the production truck outside, controlling the camera shots.

Just like in the World Cup the previous summer, this was the steepest of learning curves. For example, it was the first time I'd worn a radio headset and I started happily chatting away to Mike before being told, no, shut up, just stop. When he wanted to speak to me, it was simply 'Geoff, Mike,' and my response would be, 'Mike, Geoff.' It's something I take for granted now, like breathing, but, back then, it was an eye-opener and a world where I had to learn fast or disappear.

You had to think on your feet. Mike and I were due to do a game in the north one Saturday, but there were blizzards up and down the country and, one by one, games were being called off. Neither of us had a mobile phone at the time, so we had to stop at each service station on the M1 to use a pay phone to find out which games were still on or had been postponed.

At the time, Luton still had their plastic pitch at Kenilworth Road, so we headed back south and then had to improvise once we arrived. There were only two land-lines, which we immediately commandeered, and then it was a case of going to all the remaining foreign commentators who, thankfully, had mobile phones they could use for commentary.

The problem was, come half-time, all their batteries were running low so, quick as a flash, Mike tells me to head over to the executive boxes in one of the stands. His reasoning was that, if you could afford an executive box, you could afford a mobile phone. To be fair, he was spot on.

So, I'm going from box to box, offering £50 to anybody who would let us use their phones for second-half commentary. I got about half a dozen and then had to leg it back to the television gantry and throw each phone up to a commentator before they got back on air for the second half. After the game, it was back to the executive boxes, handing back mobiles and £50 a pop to make up for the flat batteries.

It was a fantastic gig but just one day a week, and that wasn't keeping the wolf from the door, hence the wine bar and anything else I could lay my hands on to make a few bob because I was still, basically, flat broke.

But through Mike, I met other directors who were freelancing for Sky. Now, this was before the glitz and the glamour of the Premier League and Sky were just picking up broadcast rights where they could, kind of scrabbling around to fill their schedules but also building a reputation as the new kids on the block with fresh ideas and trying to do things differently than the old ways of BBC and ITV. To me, that sounded right up my street.

At the start of 1991, I was asked to become a floor manager for Sky on a freelance basis, and the first ever game I did for Sky was on 5 January 1991, Blackpool versus Spurs in the FA Cup third round.

It was much later to become their strapline for the launch of their Premier League coverage, but for me, this really was A Whole New Ball Game.

2

New Sky Thinking

When Rupert Murdoch decided to invest £300 million to spark both a football and television revolution, I was the one person asked to give it the thumbs up before it could go ahead. I was the man upon whose very shoulders lay the responsibility of directing the course of history.

That's the truth. The devil, however, is very much in the detail.

I was a trainee floor manager at Sky, still really taking my first steps in the industry and only barely getting to grips with the job. Yet when I raised my right hand in the air and stuck up my thumb on the afternoon of 16 August 1992, I cued referee Mike Reed to blow his whistle to kick off the first televised match of the Premier League era between Nottingham Forest and Liverpool. Whenever I tell people I personally started Sky's live Premier League coverage, I obviously focus on the facts rather than the details.

In truth, I wasn't really a proper floor manager either. I was more the liaison man pitchside who'd got his foot in the door thanks to Mike Wilmot and my work with the foreign broadcasters, which had brought me to Sky's attention. I was just one of a handful of freelancers Sky used in the early days on all kinds of matches, from the FA Cup, through to the more obscure Zenith Data Systems Cup, and any other broadcast rights they picked up to fill their schedules.

What I realized pretty quickly, though, was how to make myself useful when I did get a match gig. At that stage it wasn't about talking to players or getting them onside, I was a million miles from there. What makes you desirable to a football match director and also a match producer is to be their eyes and ears. They're in the truck outside the ground and can see whatever the camera sees, but they don't have a feel or sense of what is happening away from the cameras.

To be able to sense and pick those kinds of things up and relay them quickly is vital. For example, a certain player may be on the verge of being left out of the team. Now, he may not get off the bus with a face like thunder, he might look perfectly normal on arrival, but if suddenly you see him outside the dressing room when others are beginning to get changed, you're straight onto the director and prepare him for a shot or a line from the reporter.

Along with cameramen and commentators, I would watch the warm-up intently, because you can see whether a player is feeling an injury or not moving freely so you're straight on the headset, alerting the truck for a shot of him. If a manager makes it clear he's not interested in co-operating, or is all gung-ho and up for the game, that sets the mood for the day, you get a sense of the mindset and you can relay that straight back to the director so he also gets a feel for how things might pan out. You can't actually plan for the way the game is going to go, but you can tap into the mood. All that informs picture choice and editorial decisions, but more than anything, it sets the scene.

Thankfully, I was building a little bit of a reputation as a handy man to have around, and I was getting more and more work with Sky and other production companies. It was doing Blackpool versus Spurs in the FA Cup in 1991 that I first met Andy Gray when he started using the exercise bike next to me in the gym.

At that time, I was still sifting through the wreckage of my finances caused by the collapse of my business. I was still absolutely flat broke, couldn't afford a car and was barely keeping myself afloat. So, while the freelance gigs with Sky and the rest were sporadic, I knew I literally couldn't afford to say no to a single thing. I got some work with the Football League, interviewing managers for their club's end-of-season videos. A great opportunity, my first interviewing job, all very grand. Except that it was an utterly fraught, complete seat-of-the-pants job at times.

I was asked to do Southampton, and the only opportunity to sit down with their manager, Chris Nicholl, was straight after the penultimate game of the season at Derby. The only problem was that Southampton got stuffed 6-2 so there I was interviewing Chris – who wasn't exactly Mr Joviality with the media even on the best of occasions – about the whole season off the back of an absolute hammering, while the Southampton players were all waiting on the bus to leave the Baseball Ground. Unsurprisingly, Chris and Southampton parted company soon after.

But through that job, I was building up a network of contacts. I interviewed Gary Speed at Leeds who was of course terrific, and Gary McAllister, who had played with Alan Smith at Leicester, so we had a mutual acquaintance which helped. Then there were other gigs, like the Kellogg's Tour of Britain cycling and the World Student Games in Sheffield, again through Mike Wilmot, which opened up another door.

It was in Sheffield that I met a producer called Robert Reeves who worked for Sky. Coincidentally, he'd edited some of my Football League tapes and thought I was a journalist because some of the questions weren't too bad. When he discovered I was only a floor manager (and a rookie one at that) he asked me if I fancied coming in to Sky and helping out on something he was producing called *The Footballer's Football Show* and a few other bits and pieces at the Sky studios out near Heathrow Airport. This was hugely significant for me as it meant that I would be on the inside, not just meeting up at grounds. I would be around where editorial decisions were discussed and made.

If you go to Sky's HQ now, it's this astonishing campus where around 8,000 people work. It's not a village, it's more like a small town. There's a multitude of restaurants and coffee shops, a gym, hairdresser's, multi-storey car park and at Christmas there's an ice rink. It is a fantastic place to work.

Back in 1991, Sky occupied a couple of units, and the other fourteen or fifteen buildings were occupied by other companies including the Harrods main distribution depot. If I thought I was entering the glamorous world of television, I was brought swiftly back to reality by the sight of rats rummaging through bin liners of food that had just been left outside the canteen. Well, I say canteen, really it was the biggest health hazard this side of a toxic dump, basically a builders' café stinking of burnt oil with grease-covered surfaces. And this was now my 'home'.

Sky's finances in those days were in disarray. They had debts totalling over £2 billion, they were losing £14 million a week and the losses for the season before the Premier League started came to almost £760 million. Staff in the sports department had not had a pay rise for two years, there was no stationery in the cupboard, expenses (such as they were) had been capped at a ridiculously low level, and you didn't leave as much as a biro on your desk, knowing it was going to be swiped by a colleague desperate just to find a pen that even had ink in it.

Edit suites were old and past their sell-by date, tape stock had to be recycled so often you'd record a piece, only for some random split-second of another show to find its way in. We didn't have an established work-pattern, we just made it up on the hoof for what worked, and most of the staff worked six days a week, were banned from taking holidays during the football season and would then disappear during June and July.

Even in the first season of the Premier League, Sky was still working on a shoestring behind the scenes, despite all the supposed on-screen glitz and glamour. On one occasion early in the following season, the production team travelled to cover four live games across four nights in a coach, finally finishing in Scotland for a Champions League game between Rangers and Levski Sofia. There was nothing in the budget for overnight stays in Glasgow, so they were booked overnight train tickets, arriving back in King's Cross at seven in the morning.

It was light years away from the conditions our equivalents at the BBC enjoyed. I remember on one outside broadcast queuing behind a couple of BBC production staff and barely containing my frustration as they bemoaned the absence of avocado from the buffet spread. It truly was a different world.

Despite the dilapidated conditions, working there was amazing, a real immersion into how television works and an insight behind the scenes into how a programme gets on air. Rather grandiosely, I had regarded myself as a floor manager, but once I went into Sky, I realized I was far from being that. Really, my job was booking guests, looking after them when they arrived, making sure they had a cup of tea and then taking them to the studio. I was a fixer, pure and simple – and I loved it.

Researching this book, I went through a file of old invoices I kept from those freelance days and looking at the names of the people I booked makes me think how fortunate I'd been to get a foot in the door at that stage of Sky's development. Bobby Moore, George Best, Alan Shearer, Ron Atkinson, Dave Bassett, Clive Allen, Alan Hansen, Phil Neal . . . these were all major names at the time and I was working with them, chatting to them, getting to know them and making contacts. I even got Mick Luckhurst on *The Footballer's Football Show* when we were talking about crossing over into other sports.

Some of these people are still friends over thirty years later.

To be fair, I wasn't always successful in my quest to book guests but I thought perhaps a family connection might help. I phoned Peter Shreeves, who was then manager at Spurs and, despite me telling him he was my grandfather's cousin and that was why we shared a surname, he wasn't interested. In fact, on the few occasions when I've met him over the years, he always greets me with 'hello, Gary'. So much for keeping it in the family.

Actually, *The Footballer's Football Show* wasn't just an excellent programme, it was also an exercise in subterfuge at times. There was obviously a strategy in place to compete for the live rights once the Premier League launched, so, as well as the normal formal players who were guests on the show, many of the most influential voices like Rick Parry, the new chief executive of the league, Martin Edwards, chairman of Manchester United and Chelsea supremo, Ken Bates, also found their way on.

They'd come on the show, film for an hour and then be whisked off to be wined and dined by Sky's top brass to discuss proposals for the Premier League, how they believed it would work, what they would need from any television channel involved and gradually introducing Sky into the conversation.

This was staggering to me, to be part of this life. I'd do a couple of days early in the week, Monday and Tuesday, and then later on in the week, we'd be working towards *Soccer Weekend*, where we previewed the games, tried to pull together as much gossip, injury news and transfer talk as we could. There would be no press officers or agents, your best contact was often the manager's secretary, who would put you through if you were lucky and pick up bits and pieces the managers didn't mind giving away.

Training grounds were also good targets. Places like Arsenal's London Colney and Chelsea's training ground at Harlington weren't owned by the clubs, they were rented from universities, so there was always a public pay phone there. I'd phone up and perhaps Dennis Wise would answer it – he always seemed to, for some reason.

'Hello, who's that?'

'Wisey. Who's that?'

'Hello, Wisey, it's Geoff Shreeves from Sky. Anything going on?'

'Nah, not much mate. Dave Beasant went over on his ankle but he's going to be fine for the weekend.'

'Thanks, that'll do me. Cheers, Wisey.'

And that's how it went. Something like that would make a line for the programme and then you'd phone Arsenal, Spurs, West Ham, trying to get a few odds and ends that could pull together and, as time went by, people began to get to know me and might phone up with a bit of news. It was all about making contacts, speaking to as many people as possible all the time.

It was also the first time I came into contact with one of the people who would have an enormous influence on my career. Andy Melvin was a vastly experienced journalist who had spent the formative part of his career in Scottish newspapers before crossing into television where he became a reporter, presenter, producer and director. He used to appear on screen on ITV's *Saint and Greavsie* show, bringing news from north of the border. As well as producing games for Sky, because he was based in Glasgow, he'd still be my point of contact for all their Scottish football news, and I'd speak to him on a regular basis. Soon our careers would become entwined, and he helped provide the kind of education that money cannot buy.

I was making good progress at Sky, enough for the head of sport, Vic Wakeling, to call me into his office one day and tell me he had a new role for me. From the outset, Vic was wary of me because I wasn't a journalist by training, and he was steeped in newspaper tradition, but he put that to one side and told me he wanted me to do my own round-up on air of all the football gossip and I'd be known as the 'Sky Soccer Spy'.

Man alive, I was walking on air. I already had designs on being a reporter and now, here I was, being given my own slot on a Friday night. I was floating ten feet in the air until Vic said, 'Don't get too carried away. You'll be cast in silhouette and we're going to disguise your voice because that's the whole point of being a spy.'

There may not have been too much glamour to the role, but it was a hell of a lot of fun, especially when people were trying to find out who the spy was. At the time, Andy Townsend was at Chelsea, and he and I don't have too dissimilar voices plus we both had naturally curly hair. He came up to me one day and said, 'Oi, Shreevesie people reckon I'm the Sky Spy, everyone says it's me but I'm telling you it's not.' With as straight a face as possible, I replied, 'No, Andy, I *know* it's not you,' but never let on for many years just how I knew.

But the players were so open with us because we were

new and fresh and speaking their language rather than, say, the rather staid BBC and ITV coverage, which was just highlights on *Match of the Day*, a bit of *Football Focus* and nothing much else. No gossip, no transfer speculation, nothing that both players and fans alike love to devour, and what they were getting from newspapers but not from television until we came along. Nobody could claim we were reinventing the wheel, but, until then, football on television had to know its place, and that place was a long way down the pecking order. That was madness, given how much people loved the game.

Apparently, Rupert Murdoch agreed.

In the summer of 1991, football had been at war as the Football Association were taken to court by the Football League after the big five clubs – Liverpool, Manchester United, Spurs, Arsenal and Everton – all decided to break away and form the Premier League, which the FA backed, much to the disgust of the Football League who were ultimately defeated in the High Court.

A year later and talk in television began to turn towards who will have the rights to televise the new Premier League – or Premiership, as it was known at its inception. The fact was, the breakaway had been backed and, to a huge degree, instigated by Greg Dyke at ITV, who had organized the original meeting of the five main clubs with the promise of millions if ITV got the rights. So to say they were favourite for any deal was the understatement of the century.

But when negotiations began, Sky (in the form of BSkyB) were also at the table but – given the company was losing millions every week and only being propped up by the profits Murdoch made from *The Sun* and the *News of the World* – nobody gave them a hope.

Incredibly, Murdoch and his executives won the day simply by blowing ITV out of the water with a bid worth over £300 million. Suddenly, Sky had about six weeks to put together a team that could get live football on air. And not just the live games on a Sunday and Monday, but all the support programmes, because Murdoch had made it clear this was going to be spectacular; bigger, bolder and (hopefully) better than anybody had covered sport before, let alone football. Sky was losing millions a week, so the answer was simply throw more money at it, to gamble that football fans had never seen anything like it before. They weren't just buying a satellite dish; they were investing their trust in us, so they needed to be treated properly and intelligently.

The channel was going to be run by an irrepressible Aussie called David Hill who had worked for Australian media tycoon Kerry Packer and had been in charge of putting World Series Cricket on TV, complete with coloured kits, white balls and black sightscreens. Hilly was a visionary who didn't follow a single rule except the ones that made television better for the viewer, that excited and educated them and brought them closer to the action.

His first move was to bring Andy Melvin down from Scotland and make him the football producer in charge of all the live games. Andy, in turn, brought in Andy Gray, who was assistant to Ron Atkinson at Aston Villa but was open to a complete change of career away from the game. Sky already had in Richard Keys as the main host, a vastly experienced presenter in both television and radio and whose links into the football world were already strong. There was also the masterstroke of recruiting a match director called Tony Mills from ITV, who was the opposite of Hilly in many ways but just as influential in giving Sky's coverage its unique identity.

It was Andy Melvin who told Vic Wakeling they needed a man on the inside and that he thought I would be right for the job. Somebody who knew footballers, could talk their language and who could make things happen quickly and efficiently. Incredibly, Vic agreed and there I was, with my first full-time salary since my property business had gone kaput, working at a television channel that was about to be part of football history.

My first job was to find Andy Melvin a house in Hertfordshire. When he didn't get the first one he wanted because it was either sold or rented to somebody else, he, of course, blamed me for the ills of every estate agent in history. It was my fault, and I was clearly of that type. This was to become an all-too-familiar pattern!

It was an astonishing time. We might have been new, but we were no mugs; there was already a huge depth of experience and knowledge in that core team and we were given the absolute freedom to come up with ideas, the only demand being they had to be original and they had to be exciting. Hilly even gave Andy a literal blank piece of paper and told him those were the rules. We felt like pioneers, buccaneers even.

Ideas could come from anywhere. Andy Gray and Andy Melvin were sitting in a bar at Heathrow one night, waiting for the last flight back to Glasgow. Melvin was drinking Rolling Rock and Gray, San Miguel, so green bottles and brown bottles. Inevitably, they were talking football, and Gray was illustrating a point by lining up his brown bottles in formation and moving them into positions depending on the way a game went . . . and that was how *Andy Gray's Boot Room* was born, the first programme of its type that explained tactics and how the game worked from a professional's viewpoint.

Sky was such a seismic shock to football, and I found myself at the epicentre. Melvin and I would travel in from Hertfordshire every day, leaving at six in the morning and not getting away from the office until six at night. I immersed myself in his knowledge, driving him mad, picking his brain and asking all manner of questions about television and what made a good programme or how you cover live matches as we plotted and planned. Understandably, sometimes he'd snap and say 'will you give it a fucking rest' but there was so much that I gleaned from him, even on his grumpiest days.

There was very much a newspaper mentality about Sky in those early days, because both Vic and Andy had come up as print journalists and were steeped in that passion for stories and coverage that the average football fan devoured. Richard Keys was very much of the same mind, and I think we saw our biggest challenge as providing the kind of in-depth coverage that newspapers provided but on television. The BBC and ITV weren't the standard by which we set ourselves, we wanted to go way beyond what they were offering but always with journalism still very much at our core. The simple mantra for the build-up to any game we were covering was 'what's the story?' Once you had identified that, everything else flowed.

I have to say, it was a brutal school, too. We were all massive football fans and knew we needed to work seriously hard but also made it great fun, otherwise, what's the point? If one of us made a mistake, the mickey-taking was relentless, but it was a cover for a determination to get things absolutely right. We had such a short window to get all the pieces together that there was no time for nicey-nicey; this was all hands to the pump.

The mood was 'create and innovate'. Things we now take for granted, like the clock and the teams in the top left-hand corner of the screen had never been seen before and, when they became part of our coverage, it was as if we had committed heresy, as if Sky was now insisting games should only be eighty minutes long instead of giving the football fans more information than they had before.

Then there was Steadicam, actually going on the pitch and following the players as they warmed up, which was revolutionary. Mind you, the Steadicam operator, a great guy called Alf Tramonte who is still with Sky today, was none too impressed with Alan Shearer. Whenever Shearer spotted Alf, he'd boot the ball as hard as he could at him – and when Shearer hits a ball, it stays hit. I've lost count of the amount of times Alf would come moaning to me, 'Your mate, Shearer, he's broken another bloody lens.'

But the players loved Steadicam. Within a few months, they all knew where Alf would be standing if they scored and would make a bee-line to celebrate in front of him, knowing it was going to be *the* shot. Think of Steven Gerrard at Old Trafford on that famous occasion, running straight towards Alf and kissing the camera, the kind of shot only the Steadicam could capture.

There was, however, one golden rule that could never be forgotten or disobeyed; the wrath of Melvin would descend upon anybody stupid or foolish enough to forget it: Don't tell me what I can see, tell me what I can't see. Add to the pictures.

That went for everybody – commentators, pundits, reporters, voice-overs; there could be no deviation from this cardinal rule. I have to say, Andy Gray set the standard to which everybody had to aspire because his immediate analysis could be brilliant. He'd look at a goal and tell you how the striker started his run half a yard off the defender, which brought him space, then he deliberately cuts inside so he's on his stronger foot or he's peeled off to the back post, just like he would have worked on in training all week. That's both the *how* and *why* a goal has been scored, all in a few seconds of analysis and which paints the perfect picture for the viewer.

Myself, Andy Melvin, Andy Gray and Richard Keys became a very tight-knit group who loved nothing more than throwing ideas around between each other about the coverage of each game, what guests we should invite on the show and, in very basic terms, deciding what the story was leading up to the game. Then, we'd get our heads together with the rest of the team to finalize those plans. People in the game may have been suspicious of Sky, but Andy Gray, in particular, gave us credibility with managers and players, and that opened the doors for some early success and innovation.

An example was when David Pleat, then the Luton manager, allowed us to set up in the home dressing room the day before they played Newcastle. Pleaty then sat down with Andy and talked through the tactics they would be using, what his formation and side was going to be and how they'd try and deal with Newcastle. Thankfully, it worked out perfectly for Luton and Sky as they beat Newcastle 2-0 and, afterwards, Pleaty and Andy again ran through where everything Luton had worked on had borne fruit and how the victory was achieved. That was all packaged together and put out as one programme – and it was something that we didn't think had ever been seen before on British television in such depth.

But it was our live coverage that tested us to the limit in that first season. Two hours live build-up, ninety minutes of match coverage and then another hour of post-match interviews and analysis; it was a massive task, normally reserved for one-off matches like the FA Cup final on BBC or ITV – and we were doing it twice a week for sixty matches over nine months.

Very often, before a game, Andy would lead a small production team which might also include Andy Gray, Richard and me around the ground from which we were covering the game. I remember walking to the top of the stand at Hillsborough, or the Kop at Anfield, just to witness the view from the highest point and get a feel for the ground and all its quirks. We'd often find ourselves in privileged positions, popping our heads into Anfield's Boot Room or wandering the marble halls at Highbury.

I'd always slip away down to the tunnel area where I could meet and chat with the assorted kit men, physios and press officers, who always arrived well ahead of the players but who would normally give me a steer on the mood and the odd bit of team information that we could use on air. But this wasn't just about news and gossip. I was doing my best to get to know everybody, to make sure I was a familiar and trusted face.

Of course, you can't talk about the early days of that first season without mentioning the Sky Strikers, the fireworks, and the sumo wrestlers. Yes, they were gimmicks. Yes, the twelve-foot inflatable sumo wrestlers were quietly 'disappeared' after just a few games, but the idea of cheerleaders and pyrotechnics helped establish Sky's identity as much as the games we were showing. We were no longer in the world of a match starting and ending when the referee blew his whistle, there *had* to be more than that.

The fireworks caused their fair share of problems, I have to admit. Too often, they were set up in the grounds in positions where the cameras couldn't see them. Also, the communications weren't in sync and the camera missed a rocket going up and by the time they'd moved to the next rocket, that had gone up already . . . it was a nightmare. Our poor presentation director Mike Allen did everything in his powers to try and show them properly, but it was a logistical nightmare for him no matter how hard he tried. Mike was like everyone at Sky in that he wanted things to be new, different and covered in the best possible way.

But that was nothing compared to our first *Monday Night Football* match, Manchester City versus QPR, where we'd nailed a row of Catherine wheels pitchside. When they went off, they set one of the cameramen, a lovely chap called Roy Booker, on fire. Obviously, he was far from impressed, though his biggest gripe was not turning into a human fireball but the fact his expensive Sky Sports-issue coat was never replaced. He also decided that life as a studio cameraman was safer than pitchside!

The end of the fireworks came four weeks into that first season when we were covering a game at Southampton's old ground, The Dell, and a stray, industrial-sized rocket shot out of the stadium and into the petrol station down the road, travelling at head height and at rapid speed, narrowly missing a bloke who was just filling up his motor, minding his own business. He took the two-foot rocket into the club in the morning, and it was promptly dispatched to Sky's offices where it sat on a desk as a full investigation got under way.

We might have got away with that one except, a day later, a woman whose house backed onto The Dell wrote to complain that her cat had died from a heart attack as our fireworks were screaming and fizzing over her back garden. Obviously, that was probably the time to step quickly away.

In terms of learning on the job, that first season was a crash course for me. It was also an education in working in a small team under the most intensive pressure for nine months without barely taking a breath. It was magnificent, it was daunting, and at times it could be bloody difficult, as the four of us – me, the two Andys and Richard – started to forge a working relationship that would last two decades.

A special word here for Andy Melvin. He liked a drink, a laugh, a joke, chat shows, food, everything, but on some occasions he was – how shall we put it – less than a sunny persona? Because we lived just a few miles from each other, we would travel everywhere to games together: Newcastle, Sunderland, Middlesbrough, Manchester, Liverpool. We'd leave at the crack of dawn, work at the game, grab a post-match pint with Andy Gray and – on the rare occasions when we told him where we were going – Richard, before heading south.

And the talk would be football and television, television and football, how they worked together and always what we could do to improve our coverage. So for hours in the car, we would be analysing and debating and, most of the time, they were really energizing conversations. They could be combative but that was part and parcel of what drove us to be better.

There could be the odd occasion, though, when journeys with Andy could be a trial all of their own. I remember one trip to Blackburn where he picked me up around six in the morning and I jumped in the car with a cheery, 'Morning' – nothing in reply.

'Everything OK?'

'Fine.'

'Did you enjoy the football yesterday?'

'Yes.'

And that was it; not another word for over three and a half hours as we headed towards Ewood Park. We did the game and I got back in the car, expecting the usual debrief and dissection of the game and our coverage but, again, not a single word for over three and a half hours the other way. Zero.

It was nothing personal, Andy just wasn't in the mood to talk. You had to accept that, just as in the same way he could go from strict authoritarian to being loving and compassionate. At the end of our silent Blackburn journey, we came to a crossroads half a mile from my house where there was a pub, and Andy broke his silence: 'Fancy a pint?'

After the day I'd had, I politely declined.

Sometimes, it was tough love, but the fact was, all three of the other guys cared so passionately. And none of us ever got offended if an idea was torn apart, as long as someone came up with a better one. Throughout those early years, I gained so much knowledge from Andy M and Richard about journalism and how good television gets made. From Andy G, I got the inside track on how football people think. These three guys unquestionably had the biggest influence on my career. What I brought to the group was my ability to get inside the clubs, to speak to the people who mattered and get them onside to what Sky was trying to achieve and bring to the game.

The smaller clubs loved us because they were getting more games on television, the managers and players were getting far more exposure, and they were made to feel as if they mattered just as much as the big clubs who had driven the breakaway. So, that's when you meet characters like Dave Bassett, Bobby Gould and Gerry Francis, who we gave a platform to and who loved just being part of what we were building.

Often the most challenging part of the week was finding guests. There were some people who, bless them, were as reliable as clockwork. Top of that list was Phil Thompson, who brought so much experience and insight from his days as Liverpool captain and wanted to learn the media game, to hone his skills in the way he talked about and discussed the game. If somebody dropped out, then Phil was our go-to man, until he became affectionately known as 'Bognor' – as in Bognor Regis, the last resort.

The standard of guest we got was important to us because

there was no contract to rely on, not like these days when there are pages and pages built into any rights deal, which dictate exactly what the clubs have to do in terms of providing players or managers for interview. In that first season, it was all grace and favour and establishing contacts to the point where you had built up a foundation of trust.

Even when new contracts were signed and there were clauses defining player appearances, Andy Melvin always said the day we have to rely on a contract to get a guest, is the day we should just pack it in. It's about trust, friendship and respect, and it's the only way to do business, as far as I'm concerned.

We were also fortunate in that Richard knew the likes of Kenny Dalglish and Graeme Souness from his time at Radio Merseyside, so that got us an 'in' with two supreme professionals and highly influential personalities. Often, though, you'd have to chance your arm a little bit.

Steve Bruce was a pal but even I have to concede it was a bit cheeky phoning him just hours after his missed penalty against Sheffield United cost Manchester United a place in the FA Cup quarter-finals. 'Mate, you've fucked up your Cup and Double bonus, so why don't you pick up five hundred quid as a guest on our show tomorrow?' Then I held the phone at arm's length as a stream of Geordie expletives rained down the line. Fair play to Brucey, though, he came on and didn't even mention a fee.

The amount of hours I've spent approaching guests, trying desperately to convince them to give up their Sunday or Monday night to join us in the studio at a game, it's little wonder the curly hair of Sky's Soccer Spy has now been replaced by grey locks.

Terry Butcher will always have a place in my heart where guests are concerned. We had a Sunday game at Coventry's Highfield Road stadium and, by Saturday, still nobody to sit alongside Richard in the studio. He was driving us to Coventry the night before the game, and the whole journey was spent with me going through my contacts book, phoning people up, virtually begging them to come on.

I phoned Butch and he said, in any other circumstance, he'd be there like a shot, but he had his father-in-law coming down for the weekend and his wife had gone to a lot of trouble preparing a Sunday roast for her dad. Fair enough; I thanked Butch for his time and moved on to the next target.

A few hours pass and still zilch, not a guest to be had. Not even the sniff of one. Richard turns to me and says, 'Get Butch back on the phone.' I start to protest because I don't want to piss anybody off and burn any bridges with somebody as good as Butch. 'Don't worry about it, just get Terry on the phone,' Richard insists.

So, we're driving towards Coventry with me holding the mobile up towards Richard with Terry's number ringing. He answers and Richard says,

'Butch, it's Keysie. Five hours after we last spoke.'

'You're in schtuck, aren't you,' Terry replies.

'We are, mate, we really are.'

Deep sigh. 'OK, the missus is going to absolutely murder me but don't worry, I'll see you tomorrow.'

The build-up to Sky's historic first live match between Forest and Liverpool was as fraught as I've ever known anything in television. Andy Melvin had decided he wanted to feature footage from all of the previous day's nine matches as the build-up to the *Super Sunday* game at Forest. He worked out that if there were three packages of three games, each game edited and voiced to about three minutes, that would help eat up a major chunk of time during Sunday's build-up and give the production staff at the ground some breathing space. All very sound thinking in principle.

The plan was for the guys back at Sky HQ to package everything up straight after the final whistle at all the games, edit them down to the required length and then stick the master tapes on a motorbike and ferry them to my house in St Albans where I could take them up to Nottingham first thing on Sunday morning for them to be played out pre-match.

The production team, led by Mark Pearman, estimated the whole process would be finished by about 1 a.m. Sunday morning, to be with me by 2 a.m. and stuck through my letterbox for me to simply pick up and take with me when I left home at 7 a.m. What none of us realized was the ridiculous enormity of the task facing Mark and his team. The 1 a.m. deadline came and went, and they were still working at 3.30 a.m. to complete the final package.

At 6 a.m., exhausted and probably going slightly mad, Mark dropped the master tapes off at the Sky gatehouse for a bike at 6 a.m. to make the trip to St Albans. At seven, the tapes still haven't arrived and I'm having visions of Sky's first match coverage ruined because I haven't delivered the vital tapes.

Frantic, I phoned Mark. Now, I'm not averse to a little wind-up here and there, but at 7 a.m. on the morning of Sky's first Premier League game, I'm deadly serious, demanding to know where the tape is. Mark, sleep-deprived and somewhat grouchy, promptly told me to 'fuck off', thinking it was me getting him at it, hardly surprising given the fact he was operating on less than an hour's kip. But judging by the fear in my voice, he soon became aware of the gravity of the situation.

Desperate calls to the courier company were made, only for them to insist the tapes had been delivered – which was bollocks. Thankfully, Mark is the ultimate professional and, with a magnificent piece of foresight, he had made a copy of the master tape. Unfortunately, it was sitting on his desk in the Sky offices at Osterley, about 130 miles from where it needed to be.

A quick check of the planning sheet showed a technician was leaving Osterley to go to Nottingham, so he was entrusted with the tapes and got them to the City Ground with minutes to spare. Without them, I shudder to think what would have happened had 70 per cent of our build-up coverage gone out the window.

And that about sums that first season up. Sometimes we flew by the seat of our pants, but it was always exhilarating, always great fun and always satisfying to see our combined efforts often pull off what felt like the impossible.

There are far too many people to name individually but it was an astonishing team effort and the greatest learning experience of my life. Now I look back and think we had six weeks or so to get Sky Sports up and running, and in a place to begin covering the Premier League twice a week, with all the thousands of man-hours that took. It's still difficult to believe we got there.

There were rows, tantrums and toys thrown out of prams;

there were long and often sleepless nights; equally there were many laughs, drinks and camaraderie, born out of doing something completely new which nobody could ever have said we would pull off with absolute conviction. There may even have been moments where we weren't sure ourselves, though they were never spoken of. But when I raised my thumbs towards Mike Reed at the City Ground that August Sunday afternoon, I think we all realized this was one of the greatest achievements of our collective careers.

3

Tunnel Vision

My ambition was always to become a reporter. Even before I joined Sky, I devoured newspaper reports, features and interviews from all the top football journalists and was fascinated by the language they used and how they structured their articles. For me, that was the ultimate goal, and I always felt there was an opportunity for me at Sky if I could convince somebody to take a chance.

But that was a million miles away; first I had to try and master the art of being a floor manager. I was learning on the job, picking up tips as I went along and making sure people knew I was reliable. Part of that role was liaising with the referee before the game, determining the exact time when he'd ring the bell to alert the teams, when they'd be walking up the tunnel and the exact time to kick-off.

By and large, it was all very straightforward and, in the early Premier League days, there was a degree of flexibility.

This was just as well when Uriah Rennie was refereeing. He took great delight in ignoring our signals and thought it was highly amusing to see us frantically trying to get everything back on track. Nothing malicious, just a mischievous sense of humour on Uriah's part.

Mind you, I wasn't exactly immune to bending the rules just a little when required. Back in 1994, a pal of mine, Mark Craze, twigged that bookies were offering incentives to set up an account, basically a double on two races, so we both opened an account and went strong on Halling to win the Cambridgeshire Handicap at Newmarket. It was a cavalry charge, felt like about 400 horses in the race, but somehow Halling came home in front.

We'd doubled up on the Arc in Paris the next day, but the only problem is that the race started at around 4 p.m., just as Nottingham Forest versus QPR at the City Ground was supposed to kick off. I was gutted because we carried the bet over onto a Terry Ramsden horse which had a very decent chance and that would have meant a tidy little profit. But never mind, just one of those things.

I'm chatting to the referee before the game, and I mentioned I had a bet on the Arc and he asked me if I fancied watching it in the ref's room? So there we are, with the teams waiting in their dressing rooms to be called, Andy Melvin demanding to know what the hell was going on, while the ref and I sat in his room praying for a result from Paris. Sadly, my horse came in fifth. All I remember was Terry Ramsden being so upset with the ride that the jockey was sacked before he even reached the unsaddling room. Oh, and Forest v QPR kicked off a few moments late owing to 'unforeseen circumstances.'

Not that you could get away with that now, what with the scrupulous demands of hitting the ad breaks exactly and not jeopardizing the millions of pounds of revenue that Premier League games bring in. In fact, the Premier League now has a matchday official standing by with a stopwatch seemingly accurate to a billionth of a second to make sure we hit the breaks on time.

It was in the tunnel where I thrived. It was a case of smelling a story, knowing to look for the little signs that things weren't right with a player or that the manager had the hump about something that had gone on behind closed doors. That's when my antenna would twitch and I'd either let the production truck know or have a quick word with the reporter who could use the information, either before or after the match. That was my strength, sensing a story and making sure we were across it.

The tunnel was also sometimes where you took the brunt of any grief coming Sky's way for a cable in the wrong place or somebody not being happy about some minor hiccup. I was the face of Sky down there, and it was *always* my fault. I became adept in the art of diplomacy, smoothing problems over and trying to keep everybody happy. Well, most of the time, at least.

Not that I succeeded with Howard Kendall at White Hart Lane. His side had been well beaten by Spurs and it was obvious Howard needed time to calm down before I approached him for the usual post-match interview. So, having given him some space and sorted out interviews with the winning manager and the man-of-the-match, I approached the away dressing room and knocked on the door.

Now, normally, a kit man or physio would open the door, but this time it was Howard himself, florid of face and looking like he was prepared to strangle somebody – anybody – with his bare hands.

'Howard,' I started, 'any chance of a quick word for Sky?'

The next few seconds were worthy of *Strictly Come Dancing* as Howard walked towards me, jabbing me in the chest as I was pushed, and every jab punctuated with the words, 'Abso-fucking-lutely-no-fucking-chance-whatso-fucking-ever.'

'I'll take that as a "no" then, shall I?'

Working closely with a reporter on matchday gave me the clearest insight into just what was required. Nick Collins took over the senior reporter's role quite soon after the start of the Premier League, and working alongside him was an education; not only was he an experienced interviewer with an immediate grasp of the line, he was one of the best packagers of a story I've ever seen. He could take the raw footage, edit it and put a voiceover on it and, within minutes, have something that would take me hours to do.

He was a dream to work with because he was never precious about whether he got the line or I did, it was getting the story that mattered. We soon built up an excellent understanding. If I heard something from the tunnel or on the benches, I'd alert him, and he took the information and used it. That was my job and, if it helped form part of Nick's report or interview, then I felt validated. In turn, he was never threatened by me because I was light years away from being able to do a fraction of what Nick could.

There were times when our understanding was almost telepathic. In the hours building up to England's match against Ireland in Dublin in 1995, you could just sense there was both menace and violence building in the air, a mood that you couldn't necessarily put into words but that we both sensed.

Right from the start, Nick and I both knew this was going to be a difficult night, but when the England supporters – who, ridiculously, were seated in the upper tier at Lansdowne Road above the home fans – started ripping up the seats and hurling them at the Ireland supporters before rioting and fighting with police, we knew we had to be on our game.

The match was basically abandoned after twenty-one minutes so, with no match to show, it was down to Nick and me in the tunnel and at pitchside to tell the story. It was incredible, battling through police and security staff in the tunnel, grabbing the England manager, Terry Venables, or the FA chief executive, Graham Kelly, and putting them in front of Nick before lining up the next interviewee. It was a ringside seat into a fast-moving news story that would dominate the agenda for days and we had to perform.

We even managed beat the host broadcaster, RTE, to all the biggest interviews, including the chief superintendent in charge of the police, who gave us a terrific interview, telling us what the plan was to deal with the fighting and to get the England fans out safely to stop further trouble in the streets. His last line to Nick was, 'And if you'll excuse me, I'll have to leave you because I have to deal with a riot.'

Strangely enough, twenty-four hours earlier we were

both guilty of the complete opposite when we absolutely failed to see the tell-tale signs or sense the atmosphere that something was up. We arrived in Dublin, finished our work and decided to go out for a bite to eat, plumping for a curry at a decent Indian restaurant. We didn't notice anything especially out of the ordinary until we looked around the room and realized that everybody else in there was a couple. Suddenly the penny dropped – it was Valentine's Day. We looked at each other and both said, 'Oh, fuck!' Not because we were worried people might think we were romantically entwined, but because we'd both forgotten to order flowers or a card for our wives.

Watching Nick, the ultimate pro, deal with everything that came his way, was just hugely instructive. We could be covering five games a week at times, and he was always on an even tempo, rarely flustered. Apart from one famous occasion! We were at Ipswich for a game against Liverpool, all the communications had gone down, and it was impossible to find out what was going on until seconds before they happened, if at all.

In the build-up, we knew Nick would be interviewing three heroes of Ipswich's 1978 FA Cup win over Arsenal, but we didn't know who or when. Suddenly, we see three men walking towards us, only for the director to throw to us about thirty seconds before the trio got to Nick. So he had to fill – which he did brilliantly – and as the three guys arrived, he went into his first line. Ordinarily, as the floor manager, I would have lined them up, checked the spelling of their names for the graphics and had a little chat about what was going to happen. No time for that – bang, we are live.

Now, Nick knows his football and I could see a dawn of recognition in his eyes as the three gentlemen approached, but circumstances dictated there was nothing he could do with the situation he was now in.

'I'm delighted to say we've been joined by three of Ipswich's cup final heroes,' he said. 'Kevin Beattie, alongside the captain that day, Mick Mills, and . . . you are?'

Unfortunately, Nick didn't recognize the third member of the group, Mick Lambert, who had been a substitute in 1978. It was beyond toe-curling, but Nick had no other option.

When I wasn't at a match, I would be in the Sky offices, talking with the assistant producers, coming up with ideas for guests, trying to work out how we would be covering the next game and what was needed. I was also learning about production methods, setting up camera crews and eventually editing video packages. As well as Andy Melvin, Mark Pearman would advise me how to manage a two-camera shoot, how each cameraman framed his shot, the importance of cut-aways and pausing after answers to make it easier to edit. For me, it was another vital part of my education process.

And all the time, I was working on my contacts book, upon which every journalist lives or dies. Go to a game, get a number. Go out on a shoot, get a number. Never come back without having introduced yourself and exchanged details. It always makes me laugh when people say, 'Oh, it's easy for you, you're amongst players and managers all the time.' It's not as though my predecessor simply handed over 400 telephone numbers; I had to work assiduously to get any contact I could.

Part of my job was also to act as a chaperone for guests, making sure they arrived on time, had the right clothes, all the little logistical things that could potentially derail a programme. One of the guests I was asked to look after was George Best ahead of a Victory Shield game between Northern Ireland and England schoolboys in Belfast, with me charged with picking up George at six in the morning for our flight from Heathrow. What could possibly go wrong?

I rock up at George's house in Chelsea on time, thinking there wasn't a hope in hell of him even being awake, let alone ready to go, yet before I can even knock on the door, it opens and there's George looking as fresh as a daisy, bright-eyed and chipper. We get to the airport, fly over to Belfast and not a drop touches his lips. With time on our hands, he asked me if I wanted a tour of the city. A tour of Belfast with George Best? I had to pinch myself this was actually happening.

We took a taxi and did all the sights, and it was a complete eye-opener for me. Everything I'd only seen on the news about The Troubles, all the murals and the historic sights of confrontation between the two sides. We stopped on the Falls Road and George was talking me through its history when suddenly my mobile phone rang. This was a time when Sky mobiles were relatively new and I reckon only about five people had my number, so I answered it with a degree of trepidation.

'Hello?' Pause.

'Have you got George Best with you?' a strong Irish accent enquired.

'Um, yes.'

'Put him on.'

Without hesitation I handed the phone to George, who listens for a while before answering.

'Yes. Yes. No, I don't want to do that. OK, I'll be there.' And he hands the phone back to me. My mind is running riot with potential scenarios.

For thirty seconds, I say nothing, but I'm absolutely terrified because George has not uttered a word. He's just sat there, silent. I pluck up a degree of courage and ask if everything is OK? 'Ah, yeah, that was just my dad asking if I fancied meeting up for a quick drink after the match.' Internal panic and terror duly ceased.

We spent a lot of time with George when he was a guest on *Super Sunday* and I loved being in his company, chatting football, picking his brain, and simply being with not only an iconic figure but very much a hero to me. I could also guarantee one of three things would happen on any given night with him: a guy would want an autograph and to buy him a drink; another guy would want to tell him aggressively that he'd wasted his career and be spoiling for a fight; or a woman – even those half his age – would slip him their telephone number and ask him to call. Given that he was a long way from his prime, the attraction he had for women was astonishing.

Throughout this time, I was learning the craft of television, working with people who were all huge football fans and who felt we'd previously been short-changed by the coverage of the game, and wondered what we could do to make it better for people like us. Tony Mills used a cherry picker for the first time, stationing a cameraman called Peter Tushingham (brother of film star Rita Tushingham) a hundred feet in the air for the duration of the game, only for it to get stuck halfway on its descent. Tush was stranded for hours.

On match days, I was the umbilical link between the reporter, generally Nick, and the production team led by Andy and Tony. But I was also the fixer, the runner, and the man who had to ensure that everything ran as smoothly as possible between all the departments. Having said that, ahead of what would become a memorable moment of sports television, you didn't need to be a bloodhound to smell that something was up.

It remains one of the iconic moments of the Premier League, Keegan's public meltdown in the face of Sir Alex Ferguson's provocation. 'I would *love* it' still resonates to this day, shorthand for the mind games that can make or break managers in the ferociously pressurized fight for the title.

Sky cameras were at Elland Road to see how Keegan's Newcastle would respond after Fergie's incendiary remarks, which Keegan interpreted as opponents fighting harder against Manchester United and easing off against Newcastle. At the time, there was a novelty to having a manager, on headphones, speaking directly to Richard and Andy, and that's what we had planned for Keegan post-match.

The interview room was across the forecourt of Elland Road and, fifteen minutes or so before the end of the match, I went across to check the set-up. Just as well that I did, because one of our riggers had suffered a bout of flatulence on an industrial scale. I nearly threw up when I walked in the room. God alone knows what was wrong with him, but the whole place stank like a rancid cesspit;

it was completely unusable and certainly not fit for human habitation. There was no way we could ask Kevin Keegan to go in there and talk down the line. I ran back to the dressing-room area and hammered on the home team door, which was opened by a puzzled kit man called Sean.

'Sean, I'm desperate, have you got any air freshener?' I begged.

'Air freshener? This is a bloody football club, what do I need an air freshener for?' came the reply.

I explained my desperation, and Sean rummaged around in a few of the Leeds players' bags before coming up with a can of deodorant. I don't know how expensive it was, but I must have used the whole can doing my best to fumigate the interview room and at least making it habitable for Keegan to rant down the line to Richard and Andy.

Still there was the nagging feeling that, while this was a great job and a privilege to be part of providing the very best in football coverage, I wanted more from it. I didn't just want to be the fixer, I wanted to be involved in telling the stories; I wanted to be the reporter. Sometimes, we'd take a camera into the press box after a big game, whether it was at Old Trafford, Wembley, wherever, and I'd speak to the football correspondents for a line on the game.

I was always amazed by their ability to sum up a game so concisely with one or two phrases; it was fantastic. And down in the tunnel, when we were all jostling for interviews with cameramen sometimes having to use their elbows to get the right shot, I'd been surrounded by all these big beasts of television, people like Gary Newbon, Ray Stubbs or Jim Rosenthal. To see them in action, getting their questions spot on with consummate professionalism, made me yearn for the opportunity to be in their shoes. I watched them closely, making mental notes of every aspect of their work.

In those days, Sky Sports was probably responsible for the destruction of the Amazon rainforest given the number of papers we all read. Every Sunday, there would be a foot-high pile. Andy, Richard and myself would plough through them, scouring every page for a nugget of information we could use in our coverage that day, across everything the reporters had written, using it for context and background. We were a newspaper-based television station, and I knew that I wanted to be on the front line.

So, I bugged Andy Melvin. I nagged him incessantly, telling him I thought I had what it took to be a reporter and to be given a chance. Andy, though, gave me no encouragement whatsoever, which was something of a problem because it was his decision as to who the reporters were. He didn't think I had the background or the training for it because I hadn't come from a strict, written journalism background, and so had no experience of what was needed. I also think he was wary of losing me from my position as floor manager because, without being overly arrogant, I was doing a good job for him there. It was a strange situation because Andy was a fount of knowledge on how to do the job, which he took great care to pass on to me, but he didn't want that to be my full-time role. It was an impasse.

If I was going to get what I wanted at Sky, then I had to show Andy and Vic Wakeling that I was worthy of the opportunity. To that end, I did games for Capital Radio, traipsing up to their HQ in Euston, picking up the huge blue box that held all the equipment before lugging it to a game to do score updates and thirty-second reports throughout the match. I also did a few games for *Soccer Saturday* on Sky down the telephone; anything to get some reporting experience. After one report, I remember asking Vic what he thought and he said that, while I got all the facts in, it sounded like I was reading it. And he was right, I *was* reading it!

I used to love the early rounds of the FA Cup because Sky was a lean outfit and didn't have too many reporters to spare, so I'd get to go to places like Halifax, Barnsley or Oldham and do a piece that was a bit off the beaten track. I'd go with a cameraman and do the interview, but somebody else would do the packaging and voice-over which was fine, just as long as I was getting the experience. To be fair, Andy relented, though he did that more out of necessity than encouragement – we were short of bodies when there were so many games.

Encouragement came from Andy Gray. 'Listen son, just keep knocking on the door because, one day, somebody will open it and you'll be standing there, waiting to come in.' Andy couldn't further my cause, but those words drove me on.

One of the things that both Andy Melvin and Richard helped me with was the art of the question; always open-ended to prevent a bare 'yes' or 'no' – and always imagine you are interviewing Kenny Dalglish. Kenny was infamous for being able to tie interviewers in knots. I think he enjoyed the joust, and his competitive nature would never tolerate finishing second in anything.

Woe betide any poor interviewer who started with

something like, 'Kenny, how did you see the game today?' because invariably the answer would be, 'From the bench.' Or, 'Kenny, a great game today,' 'Yes'. You had to be alert, on your toes all the time with him, and give him the opportunity to talk and expand, not close you off immediately. It was a great technique for dealing with all interview subjects.

I'd go round to Richard's house in Surrey, set up a camera and practise doing pieces to camera and interview technique with him. We'd record and then go through the tapes, with him advising me on where I'd gone wrong, how to adapt to different situations and how to bring the best out of people. For somebody as raw as I was, those tapes and sessions were invaluable, and I've still got a few of them in my office at home.

To this day I never have a list of questions written down. Firstly, if you look down at a notepad, then you're breaking eye contact with your subject and that's never a good move. Secondly, there's a danger you're not listening to the answer, you're simply waiting to ask your next question. The best interviews are when the reporter can react to something that's been said, not just follow a script. Finally, if the interview is garbage and going badly, the person you're speaking to is looking at that piece of paper and thinking, 'What's the next crap question going to be?' Again, not a good look.

But asking questions was just half the battle. I wasn't doing any live interviews at that time, just interviews that needed packaging to be fit for broadcast. I'd been lulled into a false sense of complacency by watching Nick in action, cutting pieces together, adding his voice as if it was the most natural and straightforward thing in the world. Then there was me, spending literally thousands of hours in an edit suite, running everything back and forwards, slicing a bit here and a bit there, slaving away in an attempt to make a tightly edited piece that told the story without being bloated. Editing was never my forte, and it makes me realize just what a gift Nick had.

In those early days, I'd proudly present my beautifully crafted package to Andy Melvin and tell him that I'd had a great twenty-five-minute interview with a manager or a player and that had produced a lovely, shiny six minutes that *really* got to the heart of the matter. And Andy would look at me with a mixture of pity and contempt and say, 'Fine, but our programme is an hour long, not six, so unless it's sensational – and I mean bloody sensational – it's two minutes thirty, not a second more.'

Then he'd sit me down and go through the tape, showing me where I could cut down and down and down, using only what was absolutely essential, trimming the fat and actually producing something far better for it being two minutes thirty rather than a bloated six minutes. Again, superb training.

My next hurdle was voice-overs. Now, given I have a voice that sounds like Michael Caine with a bad cold, I was over-compensating from the get-go. I thought you had to sound a certain way on television, instead of actually scripting it like you would talk to your mates in the pub.

Again, it was the early rounds of the FA Cup and I'd been dispatched to Luton, where I came up with a package that sounded like some sort of 1950s BBC Home Service announcement.

It went something along the lines of, 'Loo-TON were somewhat fortuitous to advance to the further rounds of this competition due mainly to the profligacy of their opponents, Southend United . . .' It was terrible, just an abomination, and I was terrified of it going to air which, sadly, it had to do.

The next day, Andy Melvin pulled me in. I knew the piece was going to be condemned but he simply said, 'I know you think I don't encourage you but my son, Scott, asked me why you were speaking in a funny voice? That's my fourteen-year-old boy, so if he can spot you sound like a prat, what does everybody else think?' Unfortunately, he was right.

I have to confess, episodes like that knock your confidence, but I had to go back to the beginning, work on my voice, my scripts, my delivery; everything that I needed to do to ultimately convince Andy I was up to the job of reporting, and that I wouldn't spend the rest of my career as Mr Fix-It in tunnels up and down the Premier League.

Eventually, I was allowed to go to midweek games that Sky weren't covering live, just to pick up some experience and do some post-match interviews that we might be able to use for the weekend previews. After the game I'd join the other interviewers like Ray Stubbs, Gary Newbon, Garth Crooks and even, on the odd occasion, Des Lynam.

They were all working live, jostling for position and the chance to go first because they were up against time constraints to get on air as quickly as possible. I'm under no pressure regarding the clock, so I would say, 'Guys, I'm happy to go last, don't worry.' It looked like I was being helpful, but really I wanted to study these masters of their craft, to see how they operated, what questions got the best answers and how they got their interview subjects to open up in such a pressurized environment. I was like a sponge, soaking it all in.

All the time we would be trying to do different things editorially to give our coverage something fresh. I used to love going over to Pinewood Studios and scrolling through old Pathé news coverage on one-inch film for anything we could add into our FA Cup coverage. It was another opportunity for me to show I had the ideas that could work and the ability to pull it all together.

Gradually, I was allowed to do more bits and pieces where I was the actual reporter: small stuff, but where I actually did the package and the voice-over. Quite often, as well as players and managers, I would take the 'tea lady' piece. This could be anything from a tea lady who had been at the club for decades, or the owner of the club's mascot; even someone living in a flat that overlooked the ground. Another series I made my own was the well-tried and tested 'Where are they now?' Fantastic, basic reporter training. Identify a story, research it, set it up, film it, edit it, package it, voice it. I had so much fun doing this stuff and it was real progress too. The thrill of producing packages that were deemed good enough to be part of our coverage was immense. I was so proud when the presenter would say, 'Geoff Shreeves reports'. Still, I will never forget the first time when I was actually shown in-vision as the reporter, I was absolutely made up. Being heard and named was one thing but being in vision? Significant step forwards.

So the day after I appear on screen, albeit fleetingly, I was travelling into London on the train and a guy across the carriage kept looking at me. He seemed to recognize me but wasn't quite sure. Just as we're about to get off, he came up to me.

'You're Geoff Shreeves, aren't you?' he asked.

'Yes, I am. Did you watch our show on Sky last night?'

'No, I remember my sister chucking you and you crying your eyes out.' And off he went, leaving me utterly crest-fallen at my lack of profile, except as the saddo who got binned.

When Nick Collins moved to *Sky Sports News*, I really thought I might get a shot at the main job. Instead, the powers-that-be decided they still wanted their chief reporter to have a journalistic training and pedigree, some-body who had come up via that route, rather than someone who was still learning on the job. Of course, I was disap-pointed, and somewhat put out because I was contributing a package to virtually every programme we did, and now had six years of intensive training under my belt. Now, on reflection, it would still have been too early for me. I think I may have crashed and burned at that stage. I still needed to put in the hard yards away from the spotlight.

To be honest, I could have worked in local TV, local radio, newspapers, or gone on all the journalism training courses going, yet I still wouldn't have had a better educa-tion than the one I was getting at Sky, working with guys who were not only amongst the best in the industry, but who were open books as far as knowledge and passing on experience went.

A good example of this was when I interviewed Ian

Wright and thought I'd done a decent job but when Andy saw it, he brought it to life. 'You've got him beautifully, the guys is crackling like he's pumped full of electricity, full of effervescence, I love it.' And when the interview was packaged, they added some special effects that made Wrighty look like electric sparks were coming off him and the piece jumped off the screen.

All the people they brought in ahead of me – and they were numerous over the years – didn't cut it, for whatever reason. The only person who deserved a fairer crack of the whip was Clare Tomlinson, who had joined Sky from the Arsenal media team. It wasn't that Sky didn't rate her, but she faced so many problems that it made her life intolerable and her job impossible at times.

Male reporters could easily go up to players or managers, ask for their number and nobody would think anything of it; that was just part of the job. But if Clare did the same, the suspicion was that it was for an alternative reason, simply because she was a woman in – what was at the time – such a male-dominated world. And even if a player was happy to give out his number, then there would be suspicion from his partner. Just standing chatting to a player or manager for more than five minutes brought questioning looks. It was desperately hard for Clare and completely unfair, but she battled on for four seasons and was the person I enjoyed working alongside the most as well as Nick Collins.

Another break came when Andy moved upstairs to become number two for the whole of Sky Sports, and Tony Mills was promoted into his old role. Tony had always been a huge source of encouragement and now he was in a position to give me the chance I'd craved for so long, probably from those first tentative steps during Italia '90 alongside Mick Luckhurst.

I was doing more and more pieces on my own, yet still there was some resentment towards me making the step up from floor manager to reporter. I remember breaking the story of Ruel Fox's transfer to Tottenham, which Vic Wakeling dismissed with a disparaging, 'Well, everybody knew that was happening.'

To be absolutely fair to Andy, he fought my corner on that one. He knew it was a good tale and, deep down, Vic knew the story had real journalistic merit, but he didn't want to be seen to be encouraging me too strongly. I know he and Andy had words over it and, give Vic his due, he found me in the office and congratulated me for breaking a decent transfer tale that is the bread and butter of our job.

So, with Tony in my corner and a CV that was beginning to show more than just promise, I was offered the chance to share some of the reporting duties with Clare, me concentrating more on *Monday Night Football* and her on *Super Sunday*.

I was aware there were the occasional snide comments from certain quarters, that I hadn't arrived via the 'normal pathway' and, while it touched a nerve at the time, I knew I'd put in the graft, the hours slaving away in edit suites and on motorways, making contacts with managers and players, learning on the job for years and years. I'm not comparing myself to Arrigo Sacchi, the legendary Italian coach, in any way, shape or form, but I do love his line about not having the experience of playing the game professionally before becoming a coach. The former shoe salesman said, 'I didn't realize that to become a jockey, you had first to be a horse.' Like him I may have come from an unconventional route and not had the traditional training, and like him I do possess the most important qualification of all. I can do the job.

Now it was the new millennium, I had the job I'd always wanted, and I was off and running. It was everything I thought it would be: travelling the world meeting fascinating people; talking, listening, and loving their stories and their lives. It's been an unbelievable ride, one that I never want to stop.

4

A Great Knight

Andy Melvin had declared there was only one image Sky simply had to get. Capturing it meant some delicate negotiations on the part of Tony Mills, but his tact and diplomacy meant that, for the first time, we had a camera in the Old Trafford directors' box.

The reason? To ensure that when the final whistle blew, our first shot would be the wonderful image of Sir Matt Busby, walking stick in hand, beaming smile on his face, singing along to 'Always Look on the Bright Side of Life' in time with 50,000 euphoric Manchester United fans.

Only when the cameras had lingered long enough on Sir Matt did they cut back to events on the pitch and to the man who had inspired scenes of such rapture. It was a brilliant piece of editorial judgement superbly executed by Tony.

Millsy went up to Old Trafford several days beforehand and the Manchester United hierarchy were not remotely convinced by the idea. Not only had this never been done before, but they were concerned what audio we might pick up – god forbid somebody might swear. Tony allayed that particular fear stating that the camera would only arrive right at the end of the game.

They still weren't budging until Tony said, 'Look, this could be one of the defining images of your first title win for twenty-six years and will be beamed around the world. This could well be as historic as what happens on the pitch.' Only then did the penny drop.

So, it made for perhaps the only time in his exulted Old Trafford career that Sir Alex Ferguson shared equal billing with anybody.

Because while Fergie may have inspired United's first title triumph for twenty-six years and the first of the Premier League era in May 1993, he wasn't the most important shot of the night as far as we were concerned. That honour belonged to Sir Matt, a man who had almost given his life for the club, carried it on his shoulders for so long, and was now gazing down at the heir apparent as the adoring United faithful celebrated the ultimate transformation of United, from the ashes of Munich, to once more stand at the pinnacle of the English game.

To my mind, it was the defining shot of Sky's first season. It was hugely significant in so many ways: the passing of the baton from one legendary manager to another, who would enjoy such revered status; Sky's first ever Premier League champions and, for me personally, the start of a relationship with Fergie that would bring some incredible football moments, terrific interviews and access – as well as a couple of blazing rows.

FOOTBALL DREAMS. Fleetville Junior School seven-a-side team. Yours truly, bottom left.

SOLD TO SMUDGE. Selling Alan Smith his first house after he signed for Arsenal.

LUCK BY NAME, LUCK BY NATURE.
Yet it's my good fortune to know them. I owe so much to the
Luckhurst brothers. With Kevin (*above*) and Mick (*below*) at Italia '90.

HISTORY MAN. Taking Teddy Sheringham to be interviewed after he scored the first ever live goal of Sky's Premier League coverage, August 1992.

PRE-MATCH PLANNING. Early days with Sky's touchline reporter, Nick Collins, at Stamford Bridge.

NO KIT NO PROBLEM! When Sky were challenged to a game we raided the advertising department and borrowed the strips from the original iconic TV advert (*above*).

MATCH REPORT. *The Guardian* diary column noted: 'Liverpool shirt worn by a midfielder of Molbyesque girth'. Extremely unfair . . . on Jan!

TYSON FURY. The most frightening interview of my career with heavyweight champion Mike Tyson – a very scary man.

HOLLYWOOD FC. Chatting soccer with movie megastars, Tom Cruise and Robert Duvall.

FIRE UP THE QUATTRO! One of the many fun shoots –
this time posing as Gene Hunt from TV's *Ashes to Ashes*.

TONIC FOR THE TROOPS. Taking the Premier League trophy
to the forces at Camp Bastion in Afghanistan. The platoon of
colleagues I was with were an exceptional group of people.

YET ANOTHER MILESTONE. Sky's 1,000th game:
(*left to right*) Andy Gray, John Smart, Martin Tyler,
Jonty Whitehead, Tony Mills, GS and Richard Keys in 2007.

FOX ON THE BOX. Covering a Champions League final
for the US network alongside Brad Friedel.

NEED FOR SPEED. With Sky scholar and Olympic medallist Imani-Lara Lansiquot. It's been my privilege to work with her – a seriously impressive athlete and person.

RAIN STOPPED PLAY. A torrential downpour did for a Manchester City Champions League fixture on this occasion.

The relief of capturing that image was palpable amongst the Sky crew, especially as we didn't know what was going to happen at the final whistle – because we weren't guaranteed that Fergie was even talking to us. In an historic year of broadcasting, the manager of the eventual champions had taken against Sky to such an extent, he had imposed one of his infamous bans lasting three months, refusing all interview requests, stalking away at the end of matches, making it perfectly clear we were *personae non gratae* in his presence. We may have been back on speaking terms by the time the final game came around, but nothing was certain.

The falling-out was a bit of a problem for me because I was Sky's matchday floor manager in that first Premier League season, charged with fixing up pre- and post-game interviews and features, helping to get the appropriate guests into the studios and generally ensuring our coverage was as spot-on as it could be in the face of much cynicism and scepticism from those desperate for this new venture to collapse. And here I was, potentially without any access to the biggest name in the game.

The whole situation stemmed from when we were covering United at QPR in early January. Sir Alex was demonstrably angry on the touchline, ranting at his players, at the referee, at QPR manager Gerry Francis, the rival players, basically anybody who came into his line of fire. He'd been like that before, of course, countless times, and it was obvious the switch had flicked for some reason, so it formed a large part of our coverage. Why wouldn't it?

Yet for some reason, Fergie took particular umbrage at us focusing on his behaviour. Perhaps it was because we were a new company and he thought we were cutting our teeth on him (a particular and intense dislike of his), or maybe he didn't believe his actions were that newsworthy. I honestly don't know because the match coverage was very fair.

Yet it led to a ferocious conversation between him and Andy Melvin, which ended with both men slamming down the phone on each other, but not before Fergie had said any hopes of an interview with him for the rest of the season could 'get to fuck'. The irony was that one of his sons, Jason, was working for us at the time, and one wag suggested we make Jason the reporter as surely even Fergie wouldn't refuse to talk to his own son. It was never taken seriously as a suggestion, but it could have been interesting!

Not that I was completely unprepared for this kind of scenario. Andy had enough experience of Sir Alex to have opened my eyes as wide as they needed to be. The pair of them had worked together closely as manager of Aberdeen and the local reporter on the Pittodrie beat; it was a relationship that often went beyond the bounds of the job, to the point where Andy and his wife babysat for the Fergusons, but there were still some almighty rows. Knowing Andy as well as I do, he would have given as good as he got, never taken a backwards step, but still maintained an utterly professional manner. In 1992, you wouldn't have called it a warm-hearted friendship – more one of absolute mutual respect.

So, I had insight into the way Fergie operated, how he dealt with people, the media, his players, and how he dealt with perceived outsiders. However, just because I knew all this, it didn't mean the relationship was always going to be trouble-free.

On a matchday when Sky was covering Manchester United, as producer Andy would have a direct line to me through my earpiece and we would have a continual dialogue. As soon as we caught our first glimpse of Fergie away from the cameras, Andy would immediately ask what I thought his mood was. Nine times out of ten, it would be fine, just the natural build-up to a game. But on the odd occasion, my response on seeing the infamous Ferguson glower would be 'nippy coupon', an old Scottish term for a man who appeared to be itching for a scrap, waiting to take offence at the merest imagined slight or problem. Ferguson's mood set the tempo of our coverage, and it was Andy's experience that undoubtedly kept us out of more problems with the United boss. If Fergie was in a combative mood then be on your guard.

Our reporter and the person I was assisting at ground-floor level for the first five months of the season was David Livingston. Like Andy, David had worked with Fergie in Scotland, was a fellow Glaswegian and probably even more combustible than Sir Alex – and I say that with real affection. David wasn't going to be intimidated or pushed around. As another experienced journalist and television reporter, he knew a good story, and would pursue it regardless of who was standing in his way.

The fall-out from Loftus Road lasted months. It was daggers drawn with Fergie unwilling to even countenance a truce. So, we've got virtually the whole second half of the season as a Ferguson Free Zone in our debut season. Not exactly ideal circumstances especially as, looming on the horizon, is the very real likelihood that United will be there or thereabouts when the Premier League is going to be decided, probably live on Sky.

That's when you have to think laterally and dig deep.

No Fergie meant no United players being made available, so we had to rely on United legends like Denis Law, Bill Foulkes and George Best, who were all absolutely brilliant and happy to help us out. Very occasionally we'd get the odd word from Bryan Robson or Steve Bruce, the old guard who trusted us and were strong enough as characters to not be afraid or worried what the manager might say, but that was it. Ryan Giggs was emerging as this teenage sensation – not a chance of getting near him, let alone speak, unless he was man-of-the-match and then it would only be a fleeting few words.

Eventually, come early April, Manchester United put in a series of performances that put them firmly in the frame for the title. Our touchline reporter was now Nick Collins and, as usual, we put in the request for an interview with Sir Alex more out of procedure than expectation. To our astonishment, he said no problem, gave a bravura perfor- mance and then even let us speak to Ryan Giggs.

That was it, ban over. We didn't know why his stance had changed but – as any member of the media will tell you – being banned by the Laird of Govan is almost a rite of passage. Journalists, TV channels, radio reporters, you name them, at some point or other they will have been told not to darken his door again until he decides his point has been made. It was part of his armoury, needing to control virtually every aspect that affected his football club. Mind you, even a furious Fergie had to laugh when legendary journalist Bob Cass, who had been banished, enquired, 'Alec, how long is this lifetime ban going to last?'

As the end of the season approached and it became clear United were favourites for the title ahead of Aston Villa, we knew we had to be creative. The defining final weekend of the season fell on the May Bank Holiday, when Villa played Oldham on the Sunday and United faced Blackburn on the Monday, both games on Sky. If Villa didn't win, then the title race would be over and Manchester United would be champions. We simply had to be prepared, and to have someone from the new champions speak to us live on the show should it go their way. For us, just like any other broadcaster, the thought of the title being won and not a single word from the victors was just unthinkable. Time to call in a few favours.

I'd known Steve Bruce for a while, we got on well, and we'd given him a few slots on Sky which gave him an insight into the world of television, highlighted how intelligent an observer he was and helped develop a media presence. The fact he enjoyed doing it was a real bonus. So, I gave him a call in the weeks building up to the Villa v Oldham game and chanced my arm a bit.

'Steve, can we film you and a few of the other lads at your house watching the Villa game?' was the slightly tentative enquiry, knowing Brucey lived a stone's throw from Peter Schmeichel and Paul Parker, good lads who he could rope in on the act. To be fair, Brucey was understandably wary. 'Are you joking? What's the gaffer going to say? He'll go mad.' Which was pretty much the response I expected.

'If Villa win, then we won't show it and Alex will be none the wiser,' I assured him. 'If Villa don't win, you'll be champions and he won't care. Basically, it will just be a discreet van outside your house on the day of the game, a bit like a TV detector van, nothing to worry about.'

Still understandably unsure, he agreed to go along with it. Then, at 11 a.m. on the Sunday morning, my phone rings and it's a panic-stricken Brucey. 'Shreevesie, Shreevesie, what the fuck is going on? It looks like Jodrell Bank outside my house. There are pantechnicons, cables and dishes, little trucks and people all over the place. Fergie is going to go mad.'

I managed to calm him down and assure him there was no way in the world Fergie could find out, that he was already on the golf course after claiming he wouldn't be watching the Villa game (there was no way he wouldn't be watching!) and that no footage would ever see the light of day if the result didn't go United's way. Then I put the phone down and prayed.

Thankfully, those small prayers were answered. Oldham went to Villa Park and won 1-0, thanks to a Nick Henry goal, which meant United were champions without having to kick a ball and we got our shot of Bruce, Schmeichel and Paul Parker celebrating on Brucey's sofa, with no sign of the disruption our production caused in that leafy corner of Cheshire. It was great stuff that captured the moment, and of course as soon of the rest of the United squad saw it, they all piled round to Brucey's for the party of all parties – despite having a game the next day. Most importantly, not a peep of protest out of Fergie at the liberties I'm sure he thought we had taken.

The next day, at Old Trafford, it was party time. United beat Blackburn at a canter, Bruce and Bryan Robson lifted the first Premier League trophy together, and we had a field day with our coverage, to such an extent that Andy told the network that no way were we coming off at 10 p.m. as planned; we'd keep the coverage running until we'd exhausted every opportunity. Such was the power and importance of football to Sky at the time that they just let us keep running. Fergie was great too, speaking to Nick Collins on the pitch.

The next day, Andy received a call from the great man himself. 'I watched your programme back when I got in last night. It was good.' A seal of approval that was not given lightly, even if it had taken us a whole season to gain his respect.

From then on, I have to say Sir Alex was incredibly supportive of what Sky were trying to do. He realized this was a change, that it was providing the kind of platform football hadn't had before – not to mention the huge amount of money coming into the game – and he could sense this was no flash in the pan, that there would be longevity to our coverage.

We went from tiptoeing behind his back to get the first word from the new champions via Steve Bruce's house, to Alex making himself readily available in future years if United clinched the title due to other results going their way. No fuss, he would simply drive himself to our satellite office in Wilmslow, not far from his home, do an insert down the line into our show and then out – a consummate professional.

I was always sent to do a little extra interview for use later, and also in case the line went down. On one occasion, I thought it would be a good shot if, when London threw to him in Manchester, he was ready, celebratory glass of champagne in hand. Decent idea. But on the day it was almost scuppered by the fact that I couldn't get the cork out of the bottle of bubbly (friends will tell you this is a rarity).

I'm wrestling away with this magnum of bubbly, with 'Champions' emblazoned on it, just as the Sky audience are about to join us. Three seconds before we go live, the cork flies out like an Exocet missile straight at Fergie, missing his right eye by millimetres. And so the first words our studio and audience hear is, 'Christ, Geoff, you could have taken my eye out!'

If you ask me for my top ten most important people in English football over the past thirty years, I'd put Sir Alex in first place without a moment's hesitation. Rupert Murdoch may have had the original vision for a reinvention of the English game, Roman Abramovich may have changed the face of it with his billions, but the only thing that truly matters is on the pitch, and that's where Ferguson was the absolute master.

Without him, the game is a pale imitation. Without him, there's no Arsène Wenger or José Mourinho in English football, men brought in to challenge him and, in facing up to that challenge, he took United to another level. There is nobody more combative, more demanding, more energized, more fascinating than Sir Alex.

Every time he spoke to you – or at you – it was with absolute conviction, with tremendous authority and an incredible presence. He would knowingly attempt to intimidate anybody if that meant getting a result for United. That was his only ambition; nothing else mattered and nothing was ever allowed to stand in his way.

When I changed roles at Sky and became a reporter, I lived with the adage that Fergie's not always a nice guy, but he's a good guy, which I think sums him up. It was always a challenge dealing with him, whether as a floor manager or as a reporter, understanding his character and how he operated. What he absolutely despised was any attempt to trap him or make your name off his back. For a time, I didn't like it when he used to sign off every interview with 'Well done, Geoff.' I thought it was patronizing and a bit demeaning until Andy Melvin, in no uncertain terms, told me to get over myself and accept that was Fergie's way of saying I'd asked decent questions – a verbal handshake, if you like.

Mind you, Melvin's advice on how to deal with Sir Alex nearly brought my relationship with him to an end before it had even started. I was the floor manager and Andy and I had driven up to Old Trafford together to do a game when we started getting calls about a huge traffic accident that meant kick-off might be delayed. Then we heard from our then reporter for the day, George Gavin, that he, too, was stuck in traffic.

There was no alternative, I would have to step in. I was as excited as I was terrified. I'd been bugging Andy for ages, telling him I was ready to step up to a new role and this was the chance for me to show exactly what I could do. So off I go from the truck with Andy's words ringing in my ears: 'Be firm but fair and respectful. Don't let him walk all over you.'

I get the team sheets and there is a shock, no Ryan Giggs. It's a scoop and I'm going to have to lead with that one, no matter if it annoys Fergie or not. I rehearse my first question over and over in my head: 'Sir Alex, how do you explain your decision to leave out Ryan Giggs today?'

I'm ready, mic in hand, and Sir Alex is walking towards me. I'm just about to do my grand inquisitor bit when George Gavin arrives. Correctly, George takes over and, smooth as silk, asks his first question: 'Sir Alex, as you said in your press conference yesterday, Giggs is injured and unavailable today, so how does that affect the balance of the side?' Watching from the safety of the sidelines, I felt a shiver, a sweat and a thunderbolt of relief all in the space of two seconds.

In those early days of my time as a reporter, if Sky were covering the *Super Sunday* game between, say, Manchester United and Liverpool and, perhaps, the *News of the World* had a huge back page, 'Cantona is signing for Liverpool', before the game, I'd pull Sir Alex over to one side and say, 'Alec (it was always Alec not Alex in conversation), how do you want to deal with this? Do you want to do it pre-match or post-match because we're going to cover it one way or another? The last thing you do is drop it on his toes, 'Alec, the morning headlines scream . . . what have you got to say?'

Now, he might say he doesn't want to talk about it, but I would make it clear that I'd be asking the question anyway. If I thought the story was a bit of a 'flier' then I'd tell him I wasn't going to be like a dog with a bone but if it was a big one, I'd tell him that I would be asking the question, it was his prerogative as to whether he answered it or not.

To this day, I'd do exactly the same with any other manager or player if there is a 'curve ball' that needs to be delivered. There is nothing clever about mugging people because the most important thing about a question is the answer.

Fergie was certainly no stranger to whispering in my ear before an interview, telling me to ask about a certain player or situation that he wanted to highlight. The fact is, Sir Alex is a massive interview fan, a huge chat-show enthusiast, and he loves the cut and thrust of interviews, but he also used them to get something out of it, a message to his players, the fans or even the United board. It was a tool and a weapon and Sir Alex used it better than anybody else I've ever interviewed.

He was brilliant for us on the big occasions, whether it be a title decider or a Champions League final; he didn't just front up but delivered stirring and thought-provoking words. Liverpool away always saw Ferguson and his team get dog's abuse as they got off the bus at Anfield, but you know he loved it, this is what he lived for. Before the game, he would rise to the occasion, none of that 'It's just three points like any other game' nonsense. He'd welcome the confrontation with words along the lines of, 'You can feel the tension crackling in the air, this is what English football is all about.' Brilliant stuff.

My job first as floor manager and then reporter was to try and keep Sir Alex onside. I was the one in the tunnel, not in the production truck, or in the studio or up on the gantry, going nose-to-nose with the most powerful manager in the game. Inevitably, it wasn't all sweetness and light between us – it was never going to be given the different directions from which we were coming – but one time in particular, it went spectacularly wrong.

An FA Cup tie, United versus Middlesbrough and

Cristiano Ronaldo goes tumbling over to win a penalty. A debatable decision at best, and there's been a few question marks in the commentary as to whether Ronaldo could have stayed on his feet instead of going down. Anyway, we get Ronaldo for the post-match interview and I ask him what I think is a pretty valid question as to whether he went down easily and whether it should have been a penalty.

Ronaldo is pretty non-committal – to be fair his English wasn't great at the time – but he says, 'Yeah, it was a penalty.' Job done, I think; pretty bog standard and I certainly didn't come away with the feeling that I had done a number on him. I certainly wasn't aware of the impending explosion.

I'm still in the Old Trafford tunnel when Sir Alex comes out of the dressing room and stalks straight towards me. There's no time for pleasantries. 'You and your fucking questions, you're fucking out of order,' he snarled. 'The boy hardly speaks English, you're fucking bang out of order', plus an assortment of even more colourful language.

Experience – and wiser people than myself – would suggest that in interviews, managers and players are somewhat like shop customers, they're always right. But this wasn't an interview, it was off-camera, and I took huge exception to Fergie's attitude not to mention his words. I thought he was too high-handed and I reacted.

'Don't talk to me like that,' I replied, 'I'm not one of your daft young players.' That saw the Ferguson red mist turn deep crimson and he launched himself at me physically, with only the presence of United's head of communications, Di Law, who jumped between us, preventing a full confrontation.

'Don't even think about it,' I said to Fergie, which was met with an immediate, 'Fuck off, you're barred,' as he was hurried away from the scene. The Middlesbrough manager Gareth Southgate was trying to focus on the radio interview he was giving at the base of the tunnel, but unsurprisingly he was somewhat distracted by what looked and sounded like World War Three breaking out. Di is the daughter of Denis Law, Sir Alex's footballing hero, and somebody we both have enormous respect for and also someone who would tell you straight what she thought, regardless of who you are.

I had sought and received wise counsel from her on many occasions with regard to Sir Alex, so when she found me afterwards and said that she too thought the interview with Ronaldo wasn't that great, it started a sense of foreboding.

I've also come away from the confrontation with no interview, nothing. And I've got nothing in my ear from Andy Melvin, either, which is unusual. Even so, I still think I'm absolutely in the right, that I've stood my ground and that I wasn't going to get pushed around or bullied. There was no reason why I should put up with being treated that way.

I get back to my car and the first thing I do is pick up the phone to Andy. 'Fergie's gone off on one,' I explain. 'He wouldn't speak to us and he's really lost the plot.' 'Yeah,' Andy said. 'I'm not really surprised after that interview with Ronaldo.'

Honestly, I thought I'd done a decent job on the interview, asked the questions that needed asking and got a line out of him. Now I've got a three-and-a-half-hour journey home with my boss not fancying the Ronaldo interview and the cataclysmic fall-out with Ferguson. As journeys go, it wasn't the best.

As soon as I got home, I stuck the tape on because, in those days, I recorded everything and all I can think is 'oh fuck, oh fuck.' Because I *have* got it wrong. It was heavy-handed with a player who doesn't speak anything approaching decent English and I'm piling into him, demanding to know if he was a cheat and did he take a dive? I know Fergie doesn't want his young stars, especially foreign players, exposed to that cut and thrust of the media, particularly in such a savage way. I can see where Sir Alex was coming from in the tunnel.

The next day, I go to see Andy and he spelled out exactly where I went wrong. I was Sky's point of contact and poured petrol on a flammable situation out of my own sense of wounded pride. He hadn't said he wouldn't do an interview, he hadn't banned us, he gave me a verbal cuff round the ear and I could have easily said I'd go back and have a look at the interview and, if I was wrong, say I'd apologize. Andy said he'd fight my corner but that I'd got it wrong.

Basically, I did the opposite of the fantastic advice Fergie had given me a few years before and which I've always tried to follow. 'Don't go looking for trouble, son,' he explained, 'trust me, it will find you.' If when Fergie had made his original point, however forcibly, I had backed up and said, 'OK, if I was out of order, I'll apologize,' then he would have done the interview and we wouldn't be in such a precarious position once more. Because my job is to get Fergie to talk to Sky, not get us banned.

The following days saw a huge pile-on towards Sir Alex. The story had obviously got out and all those who had felt the sharp end of his tongue or fallen out with him – and there were quite a few, over the years – were using my row with him as an excuse to air their own grievances. Perversely, I was hosting a charity auction the next night and one of the prizes was dinner with Sir Alex, and I was telling the audience what a terrific guy he is, fantastic company, so generous and a fabulous raconteur. Inside, I was cringing.

Because we're banned, I go to see Vic Wakeling, head of Sky Sports at the time and my ultimate boss. Never one to sweeten the pill, Vic said, 'Yeah, I know these things happen, it should blow over, but if it doesn't then we'll have to get someone else.' Someone else? Does that mean what I think it means? That I might be out of a job?

So, I wrote Fergie an email. I said, 'Alec, full mea culpa. I've looked at the interview with Cristiano and I've got it wrong. Complete hands-up, I've looked at what you said, how I reacted and I got it all wrong. Can I ask that you look at the terrific working relationship we've enjoyed for some time and forget this one? We've worked together well and I'd like to return to that.' No response.

Our very next game was a Champions League match with United in Rome. On the night, I had no idea whether he'd speak to us. I was in the tunnel at the Olympic Stadium when suddenly he appeared out of nowhere and goes, 'Right, you ready for that interview?'

I replied, 'Look, I meant what I said in my email.' He said, 'Listen, you don't need to say anything else, you apologized, I accept your apology, it will never be spoken of again.' And that was it. Was it a weak thing to do? I don't know, but it just felt the right thing to do for a number of reasons including admitting my error of judgement. All I know for certainty is that it was professionally the right thing to do because on that basis we can start again. Also, by this stage I'm seeing him so much at close quarters we really have struck up a good relationship.

Now people might feel I sold myself short but it's important to emphasize that my job was to work *with* Fergie not *against* him. Getting him back onside and doing it the right way was vital because he could be absolutely brilliant, adding value to Sky's coverage, every interview an almost forensic exercise in how he could find an advantage to benefit his club whether they'd won, lost or drawn. Look at what he did to Kevin Keegan with a few words; he drove Kevin over the edge and destroyed Newcastle's title ambitions at the same time.

Funnily enough, Cristiano Ronaldo was at the centre of another of my Fergie showdowns – maybe I should blame him! United are in Lisbon for a Champions League game against Sporting so Ronaldo is the obvious interview. We're in the team hotel the day before the game, all set up, and I'm about halfway through my questions when I hear a noise behind me. I never have questions written down because, as I've mentioned, that feels like you've not prepared properly and you're not really listening to the answers.

I know from experience that I'm nowhere close to the end of the interview but I can see Ronaldo's body tense up and his demeanour visibly changes. That can only mean one thing, Sir Alex has entered the fray. Suddenly I can feel him on my shoulder, so I rattle through a few more questions to Ronaldo, thinking discretion is the better part of valour on this occasion and end it far earlier than I had planned.

That's not good enough for Fergie, though. 'Fucking joke, what's this, a fucking documentary? You're taking the piss,' he hissed. 'What's the problem?' I asked. 'It's you. You're the fucking problem. Fucking nonsense. Too many fucking questions.' And with that, he basically bundled Cristiano away, leaving me and my camera crew utterly bewildered.

The next day, I was at the ground and on the sideline, ridiculously early as usual, when the United team came out to have a look at the pitch. Fergie slowly wanders over to me and said, 'Do you want the team?' Now that's gold dust so early before kick-off, so of course I want the team. 'I've got so-and-so in, so-and-so will play there but the other one's injured so he's out.'

Off he wanders and I'm joined by Di Law, a big grin on her face. 'Did he give you the team?' she asked. 'Yeah,' I said. 'Thought so. He'd forgotten to change his watch when you were doing the Cristiano interview; he was convinced you were making him late for training.' Fergie couldn't actually apologize but was trying his best to make up for his mistake.

Yet amidst the flare-ups, fall-outs, rows, recriminations and angst, there is undeniably a deep sense of decency about Ferguson, a generosity of spirit that few in the game can match. I would never have the audacity to call myself a friend of his because in football I think true friends are not always easily made. There is a difference between a friend and a contact, in that a friend will ring you, a contact you can ring.

So often I've been fortunate to witness the side of him few others are privileged to experience. Like the time we honoured him at the 'Legends of Football Dinner' to raise money for Nordoff Robbins musical therapy, a charity of which I'm proud to be chairman. From the moment he accepted the tribute, he asked who had been the previous recipients and what was the record amount of money raised for the charity. When I told him, it was, 'Right, we'll top that,' and he didn't rest until it was guaranteed to be a record-breaking night.

Although he did almost drop me into an early grave over the dinner. Normally it's a bit of a battle to get players and managers to the event because it's midweek, and sometimes there's such a dedication to the job that there's a reluctance to drop focus even for a night. But as soon as Fergie was announced, we were beating people off with a stick. We could have filled the Grosvenor on Park Lane with those in the game who wanted to be part of the night, let alone sell tickets to paying punters.

The afternoon of the dinner, I'm out for a walk with my wife, Di, just trying to calm the nerves, get my head straight, as I'm hosting the auction part of the event in front of a thousand paying guests, including some of the biggest names in football and Sir Alex's family and closest friends at an event that had cost in excess of £200,000 to produce.

Suddenly the phone rings. I look at the screen and it's Alex's number. My heart sinks because experience tells me it can only be bad news. 'Geoff, it's Alec.'

'Yes, Alec.'

'We're not coming, there's a problem.'

Panicking now, flailing around, I can't see which way is up. 'What's the problem?'

'Nothing, I'm just messing you around.' And I hear him giggle like a schoolboy before he puts the phone down. Of course, he was there, gave a great speech and raised something like £700,000 which, to this day, is a record for the event.

At the same event, for Alan Shearer a few years later, Fergie broke the habit of a lifetime and agreed to pay tribute to a player who had never actually played for him. More than that, Shearer had twice spurned Fergie's advances to take him to Old Trafford, a fact that obviously still gnawed at him.

On the night, Fergie's speech was so generous that even Shearer was moved. The respect was evident, even though Fergie had been thwarted in his attempts to land the greatest goal-scorer the Premier League has seen. 'Time and time again,' Fergie recalled, 'I used to say to my players, Shearer, Shearer, back post, don't let him bully you. But he did us every single time!'

Fergie was sensational that night. I thought Shearer would be discombobulated by this but he stood up when it was his turn to speak. He said, 'First and foremost, I can't tell you what that tribute from Sir Alex Ferguson means to me. I can't put it into words. Sir Alex said if I had joined Man United, then I would have won more trophies and medals, and he's right, I agree with him.

'Mind you, so would he.'

And Fergie thought it was hilarious.

I look back at my time working with Sir Alex and can honestly say they were some of the most challenging, difficult, exciting and rewarding times I've had in the business. He is unique in football; there has never been anyone like him and there will never be another.

Yes, the few times we clashed were difficult, but they are probably only representative of less than 1 per cent of the occasions that our paths crossed professionally. Many a time I was invited into his office for a glass of wine, or we would have a chat and a joke on an away Champions League game. He's a fantastic raconteur and has a real sense of history too. I'm privileged to have had a long and varied career in football, but I can say without a second's hesitation it would have been nowhere near as much fun or as exciting without Alexander Chapman Ferguson.

My abiding memory, though, will be of his last game as Manchester United manager. His team had somehow won yet another title, mainly through the sheer force of his personality and his unquenchable desire for success. No other manager could have achieved the same feat with that group of players under pressure from Manchester City's billions. It was quintessential Ferguson, an utter triumph to take into retirement. They named a stand after him that day, but you knew the Premier League trophy meant more to him, being with *his* players, celebrating and sharing their joy, content he was leaving on the high that his career deserved.

I joined the lap of honour with microphone in hand and a cameraman by my side, grabbing a word with the players as and when I could, not wanting to disturb their celebrations but knowing there was still a job to do amidst all this euphoria. Suddenly, I'm catapulted forward and almost knocked off my feet. I regain my composure and my balance, look round and there's Sir Alex, cackling away, having stuck a shoulder in my back, trying to knock me over, still just a seventy-year-old schoolkid in love with football and the occasion.

So, I grab him, mic in hand, for what I realize will be my last-ever interview with him as Manchester United manager. The golden rule may be to never put yourself in the interview but at this moment, I said, 'OK Sir Alex, it's been a wonderful ride, it's been fantastic.

'But for our final ever interview, you have to allow me to turn the tables and for me to have the last word. Let me say to you, after twenty-seven years or so in charge of Manchester United, it's my turn to say, well done, Alex.'

His response? 'Ah, well done, Geoff.'

He still couldn't let me have the last word!

5

Shooting Stars

'Don't worry about the noise, it's shelling but it's about a mile away so not a problem.'

To be honest, those words aren't quite as comforting as you might think when you're on a military helicopter heading towards Camp Bastion in Afghanistan and the enemy are firing rockets, not just in your general direction, but actually at you. But given the army liaison officer didn't seem overly perturbed, I decided a touch of the old stiff upper lip was in order.

It might have been an unnerving start, but it was to become the most incredible, eye-opening and humbling experience of my career. And to this day, the one of which I am most proud.

It was December 2010 and I was part of the Sky team taking the Premier League trophy to Helmand Province and spending a week with the troops on the front line.

The mission was simple, to take football to the forces and broadcast live into *Soccer AM* and *Super Sunday*.

Shoots are the part of the job I love, something wider than matchday reporting or sit-down interviews. All shoots take time and planning, with logistics, personnel and equipment factored into the equation, but this was on a scale and in a location that Sky Sports had never encountered.

We had been asked by the Ministry of Defence if we'd be interested in a tour in the build-up to Christmas, in tandem with the Premier League, supporting the troops and playing a small role in keeping up morale as so many of them wouldn't be back home for the holidays. Ours was a platoon of nine, including our brilliant unflappable production manager, Bridget Bremner, two top cameramen in Scott Drummond and Andrew Van De Waal, as well as myself and Rocket Long from *Soccer AM*.

We flew from RAF Brize Norton, into Greece and then on to Kandahar, from where we picked up the helicopter which was currently being fired at by enemy insurgents. To say this was a million miles away from Old Trafford or Stamford Bridge doesn't even come close. In Camp Bastion there were approximately five thousand British military personnel and the same number again of American and other foreign troops.

As a camp, it was about the same size as Reading and mind-blowing in scale. I only spent a short time there so I'm not claiming it was life-changing, because that would be doing a massive disservice to the soldiers who spent years fighting in a war, but it certainly gives you a glimpse of what they faced every day in the country's name.

The Sky crew had all undergone first-aid training and

what we had to do if we came under attack. The MoD had provided us with burner phones for the duration and we were made immediately aware that this was about as far removed from a 'jolly' as you would ever get. Every second of our footage had to be scrutinized and given clearance for broadcast because the enemy might be watching it and a stray background image or a misplaced angle could be used by their intelligence and might lead to loss of life.

We brought with us messages of support from Premier League players, and we put the trophy itself on Chieftain tanks, Mastiffs, Jackals, quad bikes, Warthogs, helicopters, on the wing of fighter jets and in the NAAFI; anywhere that brought to life the experience of Camp Bastion.

We were welcomed with open arms by everyone, and it was incredible to witness not just the extraordinary courage they all displayed, talking almost casually about how they risked or saved lives on a daily basis, but touching too, as they spoke of missing loved ones back home. Plus, they were all football mad. Virtually every tent was decorated with a club's flag and, when they were off duty, the troops wore their team's colours.

We were granted access all areas: going up in open-back helicopters, visiting front gate turrets, the firing range, inspecting dawn patrol and touring the medical facilities. It was here that I encountered Private Micky Firth who had on a football shirt, football shorts and training socks, along with a big gash on his shin. 'That's a nasty-looking football injury,' I said, 'how did you do it?' 'I got shot, ten days ago,' was his rather matter-of-fact reply. That one needed a re-take!

We were also invited to ride on board some strange-looking all-terrain vehicle, up and over a frightening-looking mound of sand. The officer in charge said, 'We'll give you a run on the Knife Drop,' which basically consists of driving to the top of a plateau and then over the edge for an almost vertical drop of about sixty metres. I'm in the passenger seat, all hyped up ready to go over the edge, telling the driver he should just go for it.

'I think we should wait,' he said.

'No, come on, I'm ready for this, let's go, let's go.'

'OK, but don't you think we should get your cameraman down off the roof first?'

I'd forgotten about poor old Scott, already hanging on for dear life up on the roof and certainly not going to survive a drop that would have raised serious health-and-safety issues back home.

We organized a crossbar challenge and the skill school was of an incredibly high standard. We also took part in a five-a-side tournament while we were out there and acquitted ourselves reasonably well, but the deserved winners were 34 Squadron RAF Regiment.

As the last day approached and we'd wrapped up most of the shots we needed, including all the messages home from those soldiers who wouldn't be shipping back at Christmas, we were told that two of us could go out on an actual patrol outside the camp's perimeter. Now, I'm usually up for anything but, on this occasion, I think somebody must have mistaken me for Kate Adie or Martin Bell. So, very politely, I declined the offer to potentially be shot and, in the great journalistic tradition, made my excuses and declined.

The footage from our trip was due to go into Sky's coverage of Chelsea v Manchester United but, on the day, the game was snowed off and we ended up with an hour's programme about the trip to Bastion, which was an incredible achievement for the production team. The two biggest problems they faced were dust in the equipment (we resorted to cling film wrapping everything) and military frequency jammers. You don't get either of those at most Premier League grounds.

There was also a postscript for which we were only too happy to pull some strings. Our day-to-day contact was Warrant Officer Rick Nevitt, without whom we couldn't have pulled the whole show together. As we were packing up to leave, I asked him when he'd be going back to England. It transpired that he'd applied for ten days' leave which should have got him home for Christmas Eve. He had to present himself for transportation, but if a medical emergency or strategic move took preference, he simply lost those days and that was it.

We couldn't stomach the thought of him potentially missing Christmas with his family, so we went to his commanding officer and told him we felt we needed some extra security for the trip home and asked for Rick. Sky then organized for him to get home on the commercial flight with us. I'm hoping that one good deed made up for the fact the Premier League trophy arrived home dented, hardly a surprise when it had been through the hands of several thousand soldiers that week. Concerned for the safety of the trophy, I flew home from Dubai club class with it in the seat alongside me. I had to show two boarding passes which read Shreeves, Geoffrey and Trophy, Premier League.

There was always an insatiable demand at Sky for the unusual and thinking-out-of-the-box shoot. You can't simply serve up the same old fare; it's an insult to the viewers who are paying their subscriptions. As a team, we pushed ourselves to come up with something different, and even before I became a reporter I relished the challenge, to find that angle or idea that would complement our actual match coverage. It was something I prided myself in being able to produce.

Glenn Hoddle's England side had to go to Rome in their final qualification game for the 1998 World Cup, a match Sky were covering. We had always given games titles such as 'Showdown', 'Crunch Time' or 'Decision Day', a bit like boxing coverage. I thought 'The Italian Job' was perfect for this one – a group of young Englishmen travelling to Italy to steal something precious from under their host's nose. We had several weeks to come up with a plan for our coverage when I came up with what I thought was a fairly obvious shout. I said we should try and get Michael Caine to reprise his role in *The Italian Job*. Good luck with that, was the general response, and where are you going to find the £250 grand we'd probably need to convince Caine to do it? Challenge accepted.

I went back to my desk, called in a favour and got hold of a number for Caine's 'world manager', and then sent a fax over outlining the proposed shoot. I knew it was a hell of a long shot, but if you don't ask you don't get.

To this day, I remember exactly where I was when my phone rang. It was the following Monday after the Friday afternoon I had sent the fax and I was walking past Top Shop on Oxford Street.

Not recognizing the number, I said, 'Hello.'

'Hello, Geoff, this is Michael Caine.'

Now, as well as being a great television host, Richard Keys is an even better mimic, so I wasn't going to fall for his wind-up, which would inevitably be playing out in the office, in front of a bunch of sniggering Sky staff.

'Fuck off, Keysie.'

'Now, I have had this before,' the voice replied.

'Keysie, will you just piss off. He wouldn't ring this quick, and he wouldn't ring himself, he'd get his agent to do it, so pack it in.'

'Geoff, I've got your fax here and, although I don't know a great deal about football, I'm an England fan and I'd like to do a piece with you wishing Glenn and the boys good luck.'

Suddenly the penny dropped. I'd just told one of Britain's greatest ever actors to go forth and multiply. Hastily, I simultaneously offered my sincerest apologies, thanked the great man for ringing me so promptly, went into grovel mode and did everything I could do not just to dig myself out of the hole I'd dug for myself, but also not to lose the shoot which I had asked him for in the first place!

Thank God, Sir Michael seemed to see the funny side, and we arranged to meet at The Canteen restaurant in Chelsea the next day. 'I'll be wearing a suede jacket,' he added, just on the off chance I might not recognize one of the most famous men in the world.

On the day, he was absolutely wonderful – charm person-ified, warm, engaging, and he couldn't have been more helpful. He did himself a disservice because he obviously had a decent knowledge of the game and, as we were chatting, I asked him if he'd come across many players during his lifetime. 'Well, I do happen to know Pelé, and Bobby Moore was a good friend before he sadly passed.' Like a complete fool, I'd forgotten he'd starred in *Escape to Victory* alongside Pelé and Moore.

When we had finished the interview, he asked if there was anything else I would like from him. I asked him if he wouldn't mind doing a promo, look straight down the barrel of the lens. I had even prepared a little script for him to wish Glenn and the players the best of luck for the game, saying:

'Glenn, I tried to pull off the Italian Job and it didn't quite work out. Good luck to you and the boys.'

He asked me if that was OK, and before I could stop myself, I replied, 'Yeah, that wasn't too bad, but could you do it again but really give it the full . . .' Then I pulled up short, realizing what I was doing. Acutely embarrassed, I apologized. 'Am I telling one of the greatest actors of all time how to act?' In keeping with everything else that day, his response was pure class. Completely unruffled he replied, 'You are, son, but it's enthusiasm and I like it,' before nailing the retake in one go. Not only did he not enquire as to any sort of fee, he wouldn't even let me pay for lunch. Wonderful man.

The one thing that drove us on was our rivalry with BBC and ITV. While, for many years, Sky had exclusive rights for the Premier League, we would share the FA Cup coverage with one of the terrestrial channels. Even though we had been covering football full time since 1992, they were still the Establishment and we wanted to do everything we could to outshine them over the big games. It was fun, healthy, competitive stuff, and they would have felt exactly the same as us.

For some reason, that intensified when the FA Cup moved to Cardiff while Wembley was being rebuilt. If the BBC did 'The Road to Cardiff', we hired two helicopters, one for Andy Gray and Richard Keys, the other to film it as it flew west from London with the cup on board. It was that kind of mentality on which we all thrived. There was no animosity, but there was a huge degree of professional pride in Sky's coverage being seen to be more comprehensive and entertaining.

We wanted to take the FA Cup back to the Seventies and Eighties when it was the biggest football day of the year and the television coverage would start at about nine o'clock in the morning and there would be Cup final *It's a Knockout* or *Mastermind*. The cameras and reporters would travel on the team coaches from the hotel to Wembley, and broadcasters would record every event of the team's preparation. We always looked to innovate but without losing the nostalgia with which fans viewed the day.

I'm a huge golf fan and I devour The Open coverage. One part of the television coverage that works brilliantly is, in the corner of the screen, the shot of the engraver getting ready to put the winner's name on the Claret Jug. Why couldn't we do that for the FA Cup? Frankly, I thought the FA would laugh me out of court when I asked them. Instead they welcomed the idea with open arms and encouraged us to look into it.

I met with the jeweller Emmet Smith who would inscribe the cup, put a stopwatch on him to see how long it would take to do, and then factored in the impact it might have on the cup presentation and celebrations. Then I went back to the FA, ran through everything and eventually got the nod to do it.

This was in 2001, the first final away from Wembley, Liverpool versus Arsenal, and the pressure was on us to be absolutely on our game. A cameraman was detailed to be with the engraver, parked alongside him as he began his preparations. Incredibly, the jeweller even started to sketch out Arsenal's name on the trophy after Freddie Ljungberg put them ahead in the seventy-second minute, only to scrub it out and replace it with Liverpool when Michael Owen scored twice in the last seven minutes to win it. The old expression, 'Your name is on the cup' couldn't have been more wrong. What made it worse for Emmet was that he is an Arsenal fan.

So as the game came to a dramatic conclusion, in the top right-hand corner of your screen you see the famous trophy being engraved live for the very first time, and equally the players and manager can see their name is already written in history.

Like anything you try for the first time, there is an element of risk, no matter how much you research and prepare. Plus, it's not like we could practise inscribing the trophy itself, so we were all relieved and pleased when Steven Gerrard held it aloft in victory. That sense of profes- sional satisfaction was punctured swiftly, though, on the Monday morning, when columnist Mick Dennis wrote a scathing piece in the *Evening Standard* saying it was a disgrace Gerrard had been forced to wait to lift the cup simply because Sky had opted for a gimmick in their coverage. As far as Mick was concerned, we had ruined it for the players, the fans and the television audience. He didn't hold back in his condemnation.

What Mick didn't know is that as part of my research I had timed the last ten finals from the moment the referee blew the final whistle to the moment the captain got the cup in his hands. This was one of the central planks in my case to get it over the line with the FA.

Angrily but also calmly, I phoned Mick and told him both the slowest time from whistle to cup presentation and the fastest in the previous ten years; at Cardiff, it was thirty seconds quicker than the previous fastest time. Fair play to Mick, he immediately accepted that his criticism was unjustified and offered to write an apology, but I told him not to bother. I just wish he had checked with us first for a few details.

That rivalry with terrestrial channels produced some of the more surreal moments of my career. In 1998, we heard through the grapevine that our rivals had secured the prime minister, Tony Blair, for their build-up to Arsenal versus Newcastle United. The PM was supposed to be a Toon fan and had played head tennis with Kevin Keegan a couple of years before, so was probably going to be a decent interview. We were gutted, that's a hell of a scoop to get the prime minister as part of your build-up.

Now we knew we were really up against it in the star feature stakes. Who could we get who wasn't a run-of-the-mill celeb Arsenal fan and somebody who hadn't spouted about their love of the Gunners before? Somewhere in the back of my mind, I had the recollection that Kevin Costner had been to Highbury for a game, so I rang their vice-chairman, David Dein, who did me a massive turn by connecting me to a film producer pal of his who also knew Costner's agent.

Again, in the days before email, another fax was winging its way across the Atlantic to Costner's management with, I have to confess, a fairly speculative outline of what we wanted. My research said that Costner had played soccer in high school and that he at least had a feel for the game. Dein also told me Costner loved the game at Highbury, so I thought there was an outside chance.

The word comes back from the States that, yes, Kevin is happy to record a good luck message for Arsenal. No more than that, no promise of an interview. We would have to wing it, plus we had to meet him on the set of the movie he was filming in Maine on a specific day, with no guarantee of anything beyond a solid twenty or thirty seconds!

Now I'm under pressure because thirty seconds isn't going to cut it, even with a massive movie star, not when ITV have got Tony Blair eating out of their hand. Undaunted, I get the thumbs up to go, on the understanding that this is a million miles from being a smash interview in the can; it's a punt and a very expensive one at that. But the fact is they backed me. That combination of an expensive gamble based on believing I could pull it off once I was in front of Costner made me all the more determined to get the job done.

Cameraman Paul Quinn and I rock up in Maine and make our way to the set where our man is filming a movie called *Message in a Bottle*. I'm getting mic'd up, not wanting to waste a second, hoping if I'm ready he might chat a little and we could end up with a stonking minute and a half. Not exactly a documentary, but I would take whatever I could get because all I can think of is Tony sodding Blair.

Out of nowhere, Costner walks up to us, no entourage in tow, introduces himself and begins to chat casually with seemingly all the time in the world. We are getting on like a house on fire when he points at my fly – I've got a microphone wire hanging out between my legs.

'Is that how you normally operate?' he asked. I point out that I'm normally slightly more professional, it was just that I was under the impression that he was pushed for time. 'Not at all,' he said. 'Why don't you come down on set and get some good colour shots to set up and then we can sit down and do the interview.'

Costner was a terrific host and he loved the play on words of how this occasion intertwined with some of his movies. Arsenal had beaten Wolves in the semi and were now in the final, so of course on the day Keysie introduced the piece with, 'They've had *Dances with Wolves* and now they're up for *The Tin Cup*, so here's a special fan who knows all about both of those.'

Thirty seconds became fifteen minutes in total and, for somebody who professed not to know much about our football, he more than held his own, painting wonderful pictures of his day at Arsenal when they played Liverpool, the charm and history of Highbury, the Gunners' famous crest with the cannon on it and being caught up in the emotion of the night. Although when he said how the Arsenal fans singing 'You'll Never Walk Alone' had sent chills up his spine, I sensed that might be one for the cutting-room floor.

Not all celebrity Arsenal fans are as gracious. I had an idea for a shoot with Dennis Bergkamp that portrayed him as a Dutch master, complete with canvas and easel in the background. The plan was to interview Bergkamp and then get Melvyn Bragg to introduce him in classic *South Bank Show* style, hopefully appealing to Bragg's love of Arsenal whilst speaking in his normal role of the host of the flagship arts show.

Bergkamp is smart and got it straight away and gave us a lovely line about Highbury being the canvas, his Arsenal teammates the vibrant paint and all he had to do was produce the last brushstroke to finish off another masterpiece. Perfect. The only problem was, when I explained the whole shoot, he'd never heard of Melvyn Bragg and certainly didn't have a clue what *The South Bank Show* was all about.

Not a problem; he's given us what we need. We finish with Bergkamp then straight across to London Weekend Television to hook up with Bragg. Two hours he kept us waiting before finally coming down and asking what we needed. When I outlined my plan, the look of disdain on his face could have curdled milk.

'No, no, no,' he sniffed. 'I will not be taking part in something that is either a parody or pastiche. I know my football and I will talk about Dennis with genuine appreciation and understanding.'

Now we've got a problem.

'That's a shame,' I replied, 'because we've been with Dennis this morning; we've got him shot with an easel and canvas and when we told him what the idea was, he said he loves your show, watches it every week, never misses an episode.'

Well, you should have seen him swell with pride, you'd have thought I'd offered him an England cap. All of a sudden, he was much more helpful. The piece went out, complete with the programme's famous titles and theme tune, but instead of classic art framed, we superimposed Bergkamp goals before Bragg introduced it with the words, 'Good evening and welcome to a special edition of the North Bank Show where, tonight, we profile the great artist, Dennis Bergkamp.'

From day one in my career at Sky the determination was to make football, and in particular the Premier League, exciting and glamorous. Go back to the very first advert for our coverage, played out to 'Alive and Kicking' by Simple Minds, and with a player from each of the clubs in the first Premier League season, and this was going to be football as showbiz, with far higher production values than we'd seen before as far as we were concerned.

So, when we wanted to recreate the scene from the film *Heat* for the north London derby, with Sol Campbell in the Al Pacino police detective role and Tony Adams as Robert de Niro's villain, there was nobody who was going to say it was a stupid idea or put a block on it. We were allowed to run with it. Although, I have to say even I was taken aback when the normally quiet and reserved Campbell produced the perfect Pacino impersonation. He was brilliant, a natural performer. Poor old Tony was not only beyond astounded but also somewhat daunted at how to follow his rival.

What was not part of the Sky masterplan, however, was putting players' lives in jeopardy, even though I did my best to drown one of its stars.

Blackpool's solitary season in the Premier League was memorable not just for Ian Holloway's bizarre press conferences but also the openness of the club to work with us, possibly knowing their top division journey was going to be a brief one and that they'd enjoy it while it lasted. So, I had no problem in convincing Charlie Adam that the best place for an interview was on Blackpool Pleasure Beach.

We'd set the cameras up early in the afternoon and Charlie was positioned so that we had the sea in the background and the Big One rollercoaster in the other shot, all the quintessential sights of Blackpool.

The interview seems to be going well but every now and then, I see Charlie looking slightly anxiously out of the corner of his eye. I carry on with the chat but then feel the cameraman tap me on my shoulder, which normally means he's running out of battery or the light's beginning to go, so I think I've still got a few minutes.

The tapping on my shoulder becomes more urgent, though, and I turn round to see what's wrong. He points towards the sea at the tide which is coming in quickly but still seems a safe distance away, so I tell him there's no need to panic, we'll wrap things up. Then he tells me to look behind me.

The tide has come up so quickly that we're now stranded on what is basically a small island. Frantically, we grab the camera equipment, take off our shoes and socks but, by the time we've done that, the sea is up to our knees and we're wading towards safety as quickly as humanly possible. By the time we reach sanctuary, the water is almost up to our thighs and, with no hint of exaggeration, minutes later where we had been sitting was probably under six feet of water.

As the Premier League grew and was being seen around the world, you had movie stars and music royalty wanting to be around football. For days and weeks, they'd be plugging their latest film or album, and to suddenly come into the football world and be around players and managers was a break from the promotional grind. We of course loved this and were delighted to be handed on a plate genuine Hollywood royalty in the shape of Tom Cruise and Robert Duvall before a Manchester derby at the Etihad.

Cruise, it has to be said, was somewhat out of his depth, and even forgot that he was supposed to be plugging a Jack Reacher movie, or when it even came out. Didn't matter one jot though, he was starry. Duvall, though, was absolutely on it; he'd been to almost every World Cup from 1966 onwards, had met all the great stars from Pelé downwards, and even said his favourite player was Celtic legend, Jimmy Johnstone. He even knew Jimmy's 'Jinky' nickname.

It wasn't just Hollywood who enjoyed being around football, stars from other sports loved the allure and knew that football could promote them. That's how I found myself in a suite at the Dorchester with the most frightening man I've ever met, let alone interviewed.

Mike Tyson was past his best when he signed up to fight Julius Francis at the MEN Arena in Manchester in January 2000, but he was still deadly enough for the *Daily Mirror* to know they'd get great mileage out of sponsoring the soles of Francis's boots. Whoever did that deal was no bad judge, given Tyson knocked Francis down five times in the space of four minutes over two rounds.

To promote the fight, legendary mover and shaker Trevor East of Sky had asked his pal Frank Warren to arrange for me to interview Tyson in London before he travelled north. Never have I been in the presence of such obvious malevolence and latent violence as I witnessed in Tyson; it was as if he was sizing everybody up in the room, especially me stood across from him. We both stand at five feet ten inches, but he walked in slightly crouched, as if he was already in the ring, determined to do everything to intimidate me and put me off balance even in an interview situation. There is one quote that always stood out in my mind about wanting to punch upwards because you could drive the tip of an opponent's nose into his brain. Even his lisp radiated menace.

He knew I was a football reporter and, before we even began the interview, he wanted to know about the major story dominating the back pages at the time, Lee Bowyer and Jonathan Woodgate's alleged attack on an Asian student at the end of a drunken night out for the Leeds United players. It was as if the story had inflamed some sense of injustice within Tyson, even though he professed to know nothing about football.

He was perfectly courteous in the short time we had together, but the man was truly terrifying. He had that thousand-yard stare that Roy Keane also possesses, which burns right through you, but he always seemed to think like a man in the ring, studying you, anticipating your next move or sentence. The aura he gave off was incredible; while I was never in a moment's danger, it didn't feel like that. I've interviewed other boxers since, but nothing like him.

There's always a frisson when you're interviewing celebrities, a reflected glamour, if you like, but some of the most satisfying shoots are the ones that take imagination and planning and where the whole team pulls off something special.

I have to confess, I'm a great plunderer of music videos when it comes to inspiration, and I returned to the well when producer Jonty Whitehead challenged me to come up with a piece that encapsulated Frank Lampard's all-action style. I knew straight away what I wanted to do because I'd been waiting for a while to try something out, copying a very simple yet clever technique used in a George Michael and Mary J. Blige video for 'As', where multiple versions of the singers fill the screen as if they're interacting with themselves.

I thought it was a perfect illustration of the way Frank plays, box-to-box, covering every inch of the pitch, involved in everything. We took him to a bar and shot him for about thirty seconds each time in different places and at different angles – at the bar, sitting at a table, on the pay phone, reading a paper; every conceivable shot. Then in front of a green screen we interviewed Frank in traditional style, and back in the edit suite surrounded him with himself.

Probably nobody remembers it but, to me, that summed up what Sky's coverage is all about. It's hard when you cover so many games, but whenever possible it should never be ordinary or run-of-the-mill; it may not work every time, yet nobody should be hammered for trying to be different. I love the mantra, 'There is no such thing as a bad idea, just ideas that work and ideas that don't.'

And the fact is, the younger generation of players want

and expect to be doing something different. There will always be the need for a 'straight' one-to-one interview when the situation demands it. There's no point in having frills and furbelows on a piece if we're talking about a player or manager's future and it demands a seriousness of approach. These editorially strong interviews are every bit as important today as they always have been.

But of course, times change. The modern player has grown up with social media and recognizes the importance of content creation that benefits him as much as it works for television. I must give credit to the FA and Gareth Southgate for leading the way with the England players in particular, opening them up to the idea that positive inter-action on all channels breeds positivity in their media coverage.

It has certainly given our jobs as reporters variety. Quizzes, challenges, memory tests, you name it: most players are up for it. Recently my colleague, reporter Patrick Davidson, put a suggestion to Arsenal that they not only endorsed but helped in the creation of. Patrick took Bukayo Saka back to his schooldays by showing him recorded comments from teachers who have helped shape his life and career. Bukayo absolutely loved reminiscing, fully recognizing the important contribution they had made and realizing what an important piece it was. Arsenal embraced the concept, and it provided a piece that gave great insight into the person at the centre of it.

Having the likes of Gary Neville, Jamie Redknapp and Jamie Carragher on board also helps, because they have that huge degree of credibility within the game that opens doors for Sky. I think I have built up a level of trust with a whole host of players past and present, which goes a long way, but G Nev and the two Jamies are seen as still fresh from the dressing room, which opens its own doors and provides a different type of interview.

There had to be an evolution because the audience expects so much more nowadays, not only from the traditional channels but via other platforms, too. Sky's digital reach and social media platforms are hitting thirty million plus views per month, but the central core must always be the validity of the content.

Having said that, one of my favourite encounters was purely social and not committed to film. As you will be more than aware by now, I am not averse to a bit of name-dropping and love Brian Clough's immortal line, 'Sinatra, yes, he's another one. He met me . . .'

It dates back to the 1998 World Cup in France and, for once, I'm not working for either Sky or Fox in the States. I'm only at the tournament courtesy of the generosity of some sponsors and the FA's commercial department. I was invited to England's second group game against Romania, and the organization wasn't the best, with the FA's guests dotted around in various parts of the ground. I got chatting to another of the guests, a lovely man by the name of Lance Yates. Lance explained he was in the music industry but had also bought the sportswear brand, Admiral, which was huge in the Seventies and was now enjoying something of a retro renaissance.

We got on like a house on fire and agreed to stay in touch. A few days later and England qualified from their group after beating Colombia and were drawn to play Argentina in St-Étienne. The phone rang and it was Lance, asking if I was planning to go back for England's match, which I was – thanks to one of the FA sponsors.

'OK, that's good,' Lance said. 'You seem pretty well connected and I'm concerned about my friend who needs looking after. Would that be all right?'

'Sure, who is it?'

'Mick Jagger. Would you mind?'

Mind? Was I OK with the idea? I would have crawled over broken glass just to spend a few minutes in Mick's company, given my love of the Rolling Stones and everything they've ever done. According to Lance, there would be some need for security which he was struggling to organize, and, from experience, Mick's arrival anywhere causes a degree of chaos.

My first call was to the World Cup organizing committee, who were utterly dismissive until I mentioned the words 'Mick' and 'Jagger' in the same sentence and then suddenly they couldn't do enough for me. A security detail? Of course, Mr Shreeves, and would you also like police outriders? You do? *Pas de problème*.

Mick (he is obviously always Mick to me!) arrived with his party of about ten people, including his twelve-year-old son, James, on a private jet from Amsterdam where the Stones were playing a few gigs. As they disembarked, another plane was taxiing for take-off when suddenly it rolled to a halt, the doors opened and the stairs were put out before the pilot ran over and bagged Mick's autograph, before haring back to resume take-off. That's when I realized why we needed security.

Without requiring the pesky inconvenience of passport control, Mick and his family and friends jumped into the two people-carriers I had arranged (plus police motorcycle outriders), where I joined them before being whisked off to a Michelin-starred restaurant that I'd organized not too far from the stadium. Lance asked me whether, as a favour, I'd mind sitting opposite Mick at lunch because, apparently, he wanted to talk football and I was the most qualified person in the party to indulge this desire.

Most people associate him with cricket because he travels all over the world for England Test matches and is often seen at Lord's, but he was equally at home chatting football, talking about going to Arsenal as a boy. He was just hugely knowledgeable about the whole game.

At the ground, we are taken straight down a tunnel into a private area where we're joined by a couple of guys I can only assume are bodyguards. We sit and watch the game unfold – Michael Owen's astonishing goal, David Beckham's red card – before we get through extra time and penalties. All the time, Mick is discussing formations and tactics, to the point where, after Beckham was sent off, he immediately said Glenn Hoddle would leave one up top and push Paul Merson out to the left to counter Argentina's extra man. He really knew the game.

We all watched the penalties from a vantage point close to the exit and, as soon as David Batty failed to score, we were down, into the people-carriers and out on our way back to the private airfield where Mick's plane was waiting.

At the terminal, I popped to the toilet and was standing at the urinal when Mick walked in. So, I'm standing at the urinal with Mick Jagger on my left when the door opened and somebody else was on my right – Michel Platini.

Platini looked across me, spotted Mick and said, 'Hi

Mick, did you not go to the game?' Mick told him that, yes, absolutely he'd been there. 'So, how did you get here so early?' Mick very kindly informed him that the fella standing between them, trying to have a quiet pee, had sorted a police escort to and from the stadium.

I'm not sure who Platini thought I was, but he said, 'I'm the head of the World Cup Organizing Committee and even I don't get that treatment,' before wandering off, shaking his head in bemusement.

If this whole situation was strange, it was about to turn downright surreal. Mick approached me and I thought he was simply going to say, you know, thanks for your help today, nice to have met you and cheerio. Instead, he said, 'How are you getting home?'

'Well,' I replied, 'I've probably missed my flight, so I'll find myself a cheap hotel and then fly back to London tomorrow.'

'If it's not too much of a problem,' said Mick, 'could you drop me off in Amsterdam and then you take the plane on to London with James because he needs to get home to his mum?'

So, we flew from St-Étienne to Amsterdam, Mick and his entourage departed, leaving me with an extremely tired James to fly on to the private terminal at Heathrow where a limo was waiting on the tarmac to take us on to Richmond. I delivered James to Jerry Hall, who opened the door in her dressing gown, thanked me for my trouble and then I headed home to St Albans.

Lance contacted me the next day and said, 'Mate, Mick's incredibly grateful for all your help, how do you fancy backstage passes for their show in Amsterdam?' If I thought

France was a blast, hanging out backstage with all the Rolling Stones as Mick's guest and then seeing them play was unbelievable.

Wonder if Jagger met Cloughie, too?

6

Harsh Lessons

I realize – even before the last syllable of my sentence has been uttered – that he doesn't know and that I'm about to potentially destroy this man's night, destroy it even before he's showered off the sweat of an astonishing ninety minutes in the Nou Camp. It's not premeditated. It's not meant with any malice. In fact, to be brutally honest he is the only person I don't want to interview on that night where traditionally we would mop up as many joyous players as we could.

But Branislav Ivanović is standing in front me and it's with a sense of impending doom that I have to ask the question that will no doubt inflict the kind of misery a Jeremy Kyle audience might lap up, but which is everything I hate in an interview. It's unavoidable.

It is 24 April 2012. An incredible Champions League semi-final had played out just minutes earlier as Chelsea

– ten-man Chelsea following John Terry's red card – had somehow beaten Barcelona, despite having played without their two first-choice centre halves for over an hour. Frankly, the Blues had been battered, but a Lionel Messi missed penalty and a last-minute goal from Fernando Torres meant Chelsea were heading to the final in Munich.

By any definition, it had been an extraordinary game, made even more so by the fact I interviewed JT before the game had ended – which I think was a first for a game of that magnitude. He'd inexplicably kneed Alexis Sanchez in the back, which had been spotted by the referee, and John, realizing the enormity of that dismissal and the potential damage it had inflicted on Chelsea's chances of reaching the final, wanted to get his explanation in as quickly as possible.

I'm not sure that impressed Chelsea too much, especially their Director of Communications, Steve Atkins, who, after having discovered we'd interviewed John basically in the tunnel, suggested the captain might want to 'revisit' the interview post-match. If Steve knew what was coming next, a slightly rogue interview was going to be the least of his – and my – concerns.

The madness didn't end there. We had the spontaneous creation of the 'Goalgasm' by Gary Neville, a kind of hilarious strangulated scream as Torres galloped clear in the dying seconds to secure Chelsea's place in the final. As I say, a night of chaos and frenzy from first minute to last.

There was also uncertainty over just what had happened in the aftermath of the penalty decision. Didier Drogba had given away the foul, but the card looked to have been brandished in Ivanović's direction for reasons that nobody could quite comprehend. Had he been booked? Certainly, UEFA officials seemed none the wiser, and although Alan Parry had stated in commentary that Ivanović had seen yellow, that had not been confirmed and certainly not the reason why. That was the first problem.

Now, the Nou Camp might be one of the most iconic grounds in the world, but behind the scenes it's bordering on the ramshackle. The tunnel is dark and cramped; incredibly there's even a chapel on the right-hand side as you head down the steps towards the pitch. It's antiquated and crowded at the best of times. On a night like this, it was bedlam.

Our interview position was at the point where the players have to head up a short flight of stairs as the tunnel splits, home team on the left, away team on the right, and we're in the crook of the elbow of the tunnel. Because the communication signal is so poor in there, I haven't got my usual radio where I can rove up and down the tunnel or even out onto the pitch, I'm physically hard-wired to the spot.

Ivanović had been immense, heroic even, but not really the story of the night, so hardly a problem I was going to have to confront. After all, I didn't really want or need to be interviewing him amidst the madness of Chelsea's joyous celebrations. I would have preferred him to be amongst his mates, singing, dancing, spraying champagne in the confines of the Nou Camp dressing room.

Because I knew – or at least I thought I knew – that a booking meant the Serb would miss Munich, that he'd be suspended because he was already on a yellow card going into the game.

The UEFA media officials push Petr Čech towards me, a good talker, great. Then they shove Ashley Cole in front of me, another excellent interviewee, I'm delighted. Brilliant, here we go, these flash interviews are where you capture the emotion, the jubilation, the ecstasy and sheer delight at the players' achievements, moments after the final whistle.

So, I've got my back to the tunnel, I'm about to go live, and just before I get the nod to speak, almost as an after-thought, Ivanović is added to the group. 'Oh, fuck' was my immediate thought. I know straight away I have a problem, a massive problem. To say my heart sank would be the understatement of the century.

There's no time to quickly talk to him to ascertain the facts. If I start off along the lines of 'fantastic night, what an incredible achievement', he can rightly say, 'What are you talking about? I've been booked, I'm going to miss the final.' If I say to him, 'You're not playing in the final because you've been booked, of course', and he doesn't know, then there's a problem there too. Either way, it's a nightmare.

Despite the alarm bells hammering in my head, I've got no option, I'm live on air. Obviously, I start with the other two, desperately trying to delay the inevitable, but I'm not really listening to them as I know where I have to go next. It's unavoidable. After a couple of answers from a beaming and ecstatic Cole and Čech, I know I have to go for it.

'Branislav, can you clear one thing up for us – were you booked after the penalty?' 'Yeah I booked,' he says, without any indication of what the ramifications would be. He doesn't seem particularly upset or concerned. It's odd, he doesn't seem to register the consequences. His demeanour means I have to follow up with *the* question, 'You know that means you are out of the final now?'

Honestly, I presumed he knew he was on a yellow going into the game. It's part of a team's preparation. Surely, he and the other players on a similar caution would have been aware?

His response? 'Yeah, I don't know.' There's no 'Yes, I'm gutted' or even a 'No, I had no idea that is the case.' There's just an air of confusion, hesitancy, doubt and vulnerability. He really doesn't know, hasn't computed the crushing consequences of the caution. You can see it in his eyes.

He looks to his right, glances at Ashley Cole. Ashley averts his gaze, not wanting to engage, probably knowing nothing he can say will console his teammate. Mere words hardly help at moments like this.

We are now deep, deep, deep into territory I desperately wanted to avoid, but I can't just leave it there because he has just said he doesn't know if he is playing in the final. This is the death knell for his hopes; I know that even if he doesn't.

'Unfortunately, that means you don't play in the final.' I feel desperate, I want to physically comfort him. I want both of us to be anywhere but here.

Still really without truly realizing the impact of my words, he gives the slightest of shrugs, 'Unfortunately.'

From there, it's just a matter of getting out of the interview with some semblance of dignity. I ask some question about the game – it's on YouTube if you really care about the next few seconds – but in reality I want this to end, for a player who had given so much for his club, for Chelsea fans here in Spain, back home in London or around the world, to be in the consoling arms of teammates who might feel his pain but could never truly experience that sense of loss.

Even now, as I reflect on it almost a decade later, the problems were obvious. Not that it lessens the impact of my words or the situation, but the reason for the booking was utterly obscure: ungentlemanly conduct for scuffing up the penalty spot ahead of Messi taking the kick. He'd wandered away and raked his boot over the spot and the referee had witnessed it.

Secondly, we discovered that the Chelsea manager, Roberto Di Matteo, and his staff had chosen not to tell or remind the players who were on a yellow card because they didn't want that preying on the minds of players on a booking. Therefore, Ivanović wasn't aware he was treading that kind of disciplinary line. Sounds incredible, but that's a fact that Ivanović himself confirmed.

It was the perfect storm. Ivanović's uncertainty, me having to find out, not because I wanted necessarily to be correct but because I was in a live interview and I can't *not* know because the viewer needs to know.

Did I recognize the magnitude of the situation? I think as he's giving his answer, not only am I not happy with the way it's playing out, I know I have nowhere to go. I can't go back a third time and say something along the lines of, 'Look mate, are you not getting this?' The only thing Ivanović knew for certain is that he was booked, not that he was on a second booking and, even when I told him, it was patently clear to me he didn't take it on board. It was horrible.

But you put that to one side for the time being because

there's still a job to complete. You've got to mop up all the other interviews, speak to Di Matteo, speak to Torres, put the Terry red card in perspective and reflect on a fabulous, fabulous night for Chelsea, winning against all the odds. When you are the British broadcaster, you all become Chelsea or Manchester United or Liverpool fans for the night and you want them to go through.

It was a desperately awkward moment with Ivanović, but I have to say there was no reaction from Chelsea. You know if you've crossed the line during an interview because the club tends to circle its wagons. If it had hit a nerve, perhaps JT would have come out and gone 'Out of order there, Geoff' and you hold your hands up. But there was nothing, just a load of champagne being sprayed and celebrations in the dressing room. Not a hint of the furore to be unleashed.

It was only as we were walking back to the Rey Juan Carlos Hotel, which is not too far from the stadium, that my phone began to light up.

The impact of the interview was immediate. Twitter may not have been the unstoppable force it is these days, but it was still enough of an instrument of torture for me to instantly feel its full force. I'm sitting having a few quiet beers with our studio guests, Jamie Redknapp, Glenn Hoddle and Graeme Souness, plus presenter Jeff Stelling and producer Gary Hughes, when it dawned on me just how badly this was blowing up.

Viewers are outraged over my perceived lack of sensitivity and are not slow to voice their anger. The vitriol is mixed with piss-takes, memes, gifs, and the kind of onslaught, some of it really menacing, which will be reflected in the wider traditional media over the next few days. I think it was when the Tweet from Lee Westwood came through saying, 'I've just had Geoff Shreeves on the phone telling me I've still not won a Major', that you begin to think, 'Ah, this might just have taken on a life of its own.'

And, do you know what, they all had a right. A few people told me it was great television, but they are people who know nothing about television. One of the golden rules is that you must never, ever make the viewer feel uncomfortable and that was uncomfortable viewing, without a shadow of a doubt.

For Branislav to be put in that position was, in hindsight, utterly avoidable. It's not my job, nor should it be the job of anybody in a similar position, to wrench hearts, force tears or destroy our interview subjects. Sure, never shirk from asking a question if it needs to be asked, but don't deliberately go out of your way to confront or make people feel ill-at-ease. This is football, not global politics.

The impact of that incident stayed with me a long time. Even to this day it resonates whenever I'm getting ready for a live interview, especially after a massive occasion like the night in Barcelona. I know I could have chosen my words better; I could definitely have prefaced it better. I should have said, 'Branislav, I'm sorry to ask you this because it's still really unclear. We don't know whether or not you were actually booked and that obviously makes a massive difference to the final.' And when he answers you can then be consoling and completely sympathetic.

Could I have handled it better? Undoubtedly. The one thing that still irks and is still something of an open wound is some people believe I did it deliberately, to confront and kick a man when he was down, to hammer him at his lowest ebb. Nothing could be further from the truth.

I cannot stand car-crash television and that's what that interview was. Also, I've always disliked it when people tell me I'm not afraid to ask the tough question. It's a well-meant compliment, I guess, but I really dislike the whole expression. On the rare occasion you are being complimented about an interview, it should be that you asked the *right* question. Otherwise, you're making the question about yourself – look at me, asking this tough question, and I really don't care what the answer is, I'm just showboating to show how brave I am at asking the hard question. That, for me, is not good television.

When faced with, say, a manager walking towards you whose team has just lost heavily, or even been relegated that day, you could challenge him, you can be confrontational, you can demand explanations, you can be on the front foot ready to hit him with your hardest line of questioning.

Or you can assess his mood and the situation, and never *ever* forget the most important thing about any question is the answer. Perhaps start with 'Horrible day for you, X, what are your immediate thoughts?' There are so many factors in deciding what you say and how you choose to say it, but the overriding factor has to be what approach elicits the best response.

I guess it's like being a bowler in cricket, not because you're looking to catch people out but because you have to mix up your deliveries. Sometimes it's short and sharp, sometimes it's flighted up, a bit flowery, maybe a bit overlong, but you don't bowl to every batsman in the same way. It's finding the right words and style for the person in front of you.

Your own demeanour is important, too, your own body language. Try and put the person at ease, or reassure them if the situation requires. Clarify any issues before you start, tell them if there is something left of field coming. In short, the complete opposite of what happened in the Nou Camp!

Does all that matter when you become infamous for *that* interview? Not to the critics who don't know the full story but, as we say in television, 'If you put your head above the parapet, you're there to be shot at.' With regard to the critics early in my career, I used to be quite thin-skinned, but then my pal Gary Newbon, who not only is one of the most experienced sports reporters around but also has the hide of a rhino, pulled me to one side and said, 'Listen, as long as they spell your name right and use an old photo, who cares?' Fair point!

Fortunately, I was able to repair any damage that might have been done pretty quickly. I used to present a phone-in programme called *You're On Sky Sports*. My co-host was Chloe Everton, who was friends with Ivanović and she got me his phone number. She told me he was really embarrassed and didn't enjoy the spotlight or the fuss that was still going on from the interview, and that all he wanted to do was put it to bed and get on with his life.

A week or so after Barcelona, I rang him and said, 'Brana, I'm embarrassed too, I feel dreadful that I put you in this situation. I'm really sorry.' And he just told me there was no problem, that he'd come to terms with missing the final and reassured me there were no recriminations or ill-feelings from his side. That helped me privately.

There was also zero backlash from anybody at Chelsea, other than their fans. In fact, we covered the final the following month and I put together one of the pre-match pieces that I was most proud of. You're in competition with other broadcasters and it's a challenge to keep coming up with a fresh approach, something different, something that the players will enjoy and will hopefully make good television.

You get one day in the build-up where all the players are available for interview. You can throw money at equipment, at celebrity guests, basically anything that you want. I think I spent about three quid in a charity shop in Cobham High Street, just round the corner from the Chelsea training ground, and bought an old trilby hat.

In it I put all the names of the players, the manager and his staff. Then, as the players came off the training pitch, instead of sitting them down and getting all the lighting and the sound sorted, I simply asked them to pull out a name. If they got their own name, back in it went and they pulled out another. Then it was a simple question: Tell me, in all honesty, the best thing about them and the worst thing about them. It went down a storm. The players loved it because it was a laugh and relieved a little bit of pressure that comes from these kind of media days. Frank Lampard was the star. He pulled out Robbie Di Matteo's name and said, 'Best thing about him? He picks me!'

It's only now, a decade afterwards, that I think I've been able to draw a line under the whole incident. Branislav gave an interview to Alyson Rudd of *The Times* where he said, 'Honestly, I was in shock about the whole situation. Our coaching staff and Roberto Di Matteo did not tell us before the game who was in the danger zone. When I got booked, after the game I was only thinking about the final. When Geoff surprised me, I wasn't even thinking in my head about the final, I was celebrating the semi-final and a big victory.

'I looked strange in that moment. Even when I got into the dressing room I was celebrating and happy. I realized probably on the bus when I calmed down and found out. I looked on my phone and I found I couldn't play in the final. But I don't have any problem with Geoff, I spoke with him and it was fine.'

In the light of that, what people said about me at the time and what they still say even now doesn't overly bother me. If they think I'm the man who shot Bambi's mother, so be it. But the misconception I did it deliberately is just plain wrong.

Thankfully, the moments in interviews when my blood has run cold are few and far between, but unfortunately it's happened when the occasion demanded something much better than I produced. Ivanović was one instance; another was when I was interviewing Glenn Hoddle.

I had known Glenn for some time, probably since he took over as manager of Swindon back in the early Nineties and then guided the club into the Premier League. That friendship grew when he became Chelsea manager, and we shared a passion for music as well as talking shop. It was fair to say, he had more time and trust for the broadcast media when he became England manager in 1996 than he did for the print boys who he viewed with suspicion.

In 1997, Sky covered Le Tournoi in France, which was preparation for the World Cup the following year. England were trying out the base they had chosen in La Baule. It was a fairly relaxed atmosphere and, as well as Hoddle, I knew a lot of the team – players like Alan Shearer, Teddy Sheringham and Tony Adams – and we were welcomed into the camp, building relationships and getting some good stuff.

I had also built a strong relationship with Hoddle's agent, Dennis Roach, and it was this understanding that gave me the kind of 'in' I needed when it all turned horribly sour for Glenn after the 1998 World Cup. England had lost to Argentina, David Beckham had been sent off, and Glenn had co-operated on a diary of the tournament which had caused rifts in the England camp, especially with the likes of Adams and Teddy Sheringham, who saw it as a betrayal of trust.

By the time the qualifying games for Euro 2000 had started, Hoddle and the FA decided the time was probably right to give an interview in order to redress the balance of negative publicity that had begun to surround him. The upshot was the granting of an interview with Matt Dickinson of *The Times*.

Now, I'm taking no sides on this one. I know Matt, I like and respect him as a superb award-winning journalist, and he insists he quoted Hoddle absolutely accurately on his views on reincarnation and disabled people paying the price for sins in a previous life. Equally, Glenn claims those were not his words and he steadfastly refuses to alter that position. As I say, I'm not taking sides; both men believe absolutely in their respective positions.

What I do know is that it left Hoddle in a desperate situation, with calls for him to resign or be sacked, and even Tony Blair declaring the England manager's position untenable. In the midst of this madness, the Hoddle camp were circling the wagons and decided they wanted to do two interviews to put his side of the story. He was fighting for his job, without doubt.

The first was with ITV, who nominated Sir Trevor McDonald as their man for the interview. The other was with *Sky News*, but the only stipulation was that I did the piece because of the relationship I'd built with Glenn, Dennis Roach and Glenn's lawyer, Peter Baines who, coincidentally, had bought my parents' house. In my role as fixer, I shouldn't really have been anywhere near the interview but, because I had badgered away to get it, the decision was taken I should be the man to grill Glenn.

Was that the right decision? No, definitely not. There were people in the Sky organization who were far more qualified to do the job, with more experience and a greater appreciation of the gravitas of the situation and what was required to get the very best from the interview. Call it over-confidence, call it arrogance, but I was not about to give this opportunity up. I had fought to get Sky to the table, and I wasn't about to hand it over to somebody else, no matter who they were. I was headstrong and didn't recognize the enormity of the situation in which I found myself.

If the same situation was playing out today, I would back myself 100 per cent to do the job properly and get what was needed. Back then, I was raw and inexperienced. Even though I had done a good few interviews at training grounds, they were ones that I could take my time over and package properly into the smooth product that went on air. This was different; this time I had to become an inquisitor and, frankly, I was out of my comfort zone. Plus I liked – and still like – Glenn enormously as a bloke. With me he had been generous with his time, helpful with interviews and basically just open. I remember going to a children's hospice called Rainbow House with him, and he was so struck by the incredible work the people there did in tragic circumstances that he wrote out a cheque there and then to support their efforts.

I arrived at the interview venue, and it was surrounded by television trucks, photographers on ladders and dozens of reporters, all hoping for a shot of the beleaguered England manager and maybe grab a word with him. It was clear to me this was a story of international interest, that one of the most high-profile football figures was fighting for his job and fighting for his very reputation.

Sir Trevor went first, and I watched from our Sky truck as he demonstrated all the deftness of touch, intelligence and intuition gathered from decades reporting on the biggest stories from around the world, as well as hosting *News at Ten* for many years. It was a masterclass of the art of the interview.

When he had finished, I left the truck and walked towards the front door of the house where Glenn, Dennis, Peter and somebody from the FA were holed up. Sir Trevor emerged and we passed each other like batsmen walking to and from the wicket. As he came towards me, I introduced myself, we shook hands before Sir Trevor uttered the words I will never forget.

'I don't know, Geoff, Glenn and this reincarnation, it will be the fucking death of him.'

To this day, I swear I don't know whether the situation had gone completely over Sir Trevor's head, or it was just a brilliant irony from the consummate wordsmith.

Then it was my turn in front of Glenn.

It wasn't that I didn't take it seriously, of course I did, but basically my whole mindset was wrong. This wasn't the time for Mr Fix-It from the tunnel, friendly and affable, laugh and a joke, defuse any situation with a gag; this was so very different and out of my comfort zone. I didn't judge the situation properly. I wasn't detached because I wanted to be on Glenn's side – to protect him, almost.

My questions were all wrong. I started with *'They're saying this about you, Glenn.'* Or, *'They* say you said this.' The tone was wrong, as if I wanted to fight Glenn's corner for him, instead of simply asking, 'Did you say this, Glenn?' and, 'If you didn't say that, what are your beliefs?' I didn't quite blame the media or Matt Dickinson for the whole situation, but it was pretty close to that. And it was poor.

I knew as the interview was progressing that I was scrambling, that I wasn't getting to the heart of the enormity of the situation, that I was inexperienced and not able to get back on track. The stupid thing was that I'd watched Sir Trevor, I knew the questions I ought to be asking but, somehow, I just couldn't get to where the interview needed to go.

Perhaps it was fear. Perhaps it was just not being up to the job. There have been times when, in later years and with experience under my belt, people have asked me to do an interview because they're in a precarious position and need a familiar face to try and turn things around. I've always said yes but with one caveat: if they're not prepared to answer the questions I need to ask to do my job properly, then it's not one for me. To be fair, the interviews go ahead on that basis, and everybody comes away happy.

How do I reflect on the whole episode now? I had done an incredible job of securing an interview of national and international interest, but I had done an incredibly bad job of conducting it. It was the supreme example of being a brilliant foot-in-the-door man, but then not knowing what to do when the door opened. There is no question that my affection for Glenn was the root of my misjudgement which, combined with my lack of experience, produced such a poor result and missed opportunity. It hurt me for a long while, denting my confidence and damaging my aspirations to be taken seriously as a reporter.

And it's strange when you emerge from an interview like that which has obviously gone so badly. It's not colleagues saying, 'You should have asked this' or 'You should have pushed him on that', it's the silence; the horrible indifference to what you've produced.

What's worse, it was me going out on my own with this. Because it was for *Sky News*, I didn't speak to Andy Melvin or Richard Keys and take on their advice; this was me out there alone. I didn't – or couldn't – change my role from being a facilitator to a hard-nosed interviewer and I froze, unable to put the direct questions to Glenn. The irony is not lost on me that I actually did Glenn's cause no favours whatsoever either. He had, and still to this day has, absolutely no doubts about what he said and what he believes. By not confronting him with the accusations clearly, I denied him the opportunity to reject them.

Years later, I made a documentary of his life and covered everything, all the Matt Dickinson stuff, and he answered it all superbly and didn't object to any line of questioning.

Inevitably, there was stick from many quarters over the interview, much of it justified but some of it driven by envy, I believe, because every journalist I know would have killed for that interview. I had to take it, though, I had no choice.

Shortly after the interview, Glenn lost his job. I'm not sure any interview could have saved him, not when the prime minister has gone on national television to say he should be sacked. Thankfully, there were no recriminations from Glenn or his camp. In fact, I celebrated my fortieth birthday in Azerbaijan drinking warm champagne with him and Martin Tyler and we have remained firm friends. He went on to be a regular studio guest for Sky, as well as being an informed co-commentator with his excellent reading of the game.

Like many people in football I was hugely relieved when he survived his heart attack, although I waited until he had been given the all-clear before sending a message of support. Although his life was no longer in danger, there were concerns about memory loss. My text simply said: 'Glad you are OK, don't forget you owe me £500 . . .'

In the same vein, I have huge regrets over the way I treated Danny Wilson when he was manager of Sheffield Wednesday. It was in complete contrast to the Hoddle episode, where I was far too conciliatory and sympathetic, without the instincts needed for a good interviewer. With

Danny, I was hard, heartless and, regrettably, lacking any ounce of empathy.

It was September 1999 and Sir Bobby Robson's first home match as Newcastle manager. St James's Park was absolutely buzzing as one of their Geordie sons finally came home to lead them out of the wilderness. It was one of those occasions that you feel the emotion deep inside you, even before the game has kicked off: thousands of devoted Geordies welcoming Sir Bobby back to where he belonged after too many years away.

And how Newcastle reacted. Wednesday were hapless victims, blown away 8-0, with Shearer scoring five and the Toon in utterly irresistible form. It was a riot, one of those days when nothing Wednesday did came off and where everything Newcastle tried hit the back of the net.

The story was all about the return of the native, the manager who could inspire his side after a mere few days in the job. It should have been a privilege to be there, but my shoddy performance is the one thing that sticks in my mind, not Newcastle's brilliance or Sir Bobby's pride.

It was in the days before I was the sole touchline reporter and, while I can't remember who I split the duties with, I was the man to interview the Wednesday manager, Danny Wilson. Looking back now, it wasn't that I particularly asked the wrong questions and, journalistically, they were spot on. What I displayed was a complete lack of touch and empathy, going in two-footed when all it needed was a comforting smile and a show of sympathy.

I can't remember whether I asked him if he was considering his position, but it was along those lines. Instead of saying to him, 'Danny, dreadful for day for you and your team, can you find the words to describe what happened?' I hit him with, 'You've just been beaten 8-0, how do you explain that?'

We've all had awful days at the office, days we want to forget. The last thing you need is somebody coming up to you and demanding to know why you're so awful and what you're going to do to stop being so awful.

Frighteningly, I didn't think I'd done anything wrong. It wasn't until Keysie and Andy pulled me afterwards and said, 'Jesus, you didn't do Danny any favours there, did you?' Only then did I realize the guy had come out of his own volition, accepted he needed to answer questions, and all I'd done was stick the boot in when he was no doubt at his lowest ebb. It was incorrect, impolite and insensitive.

Beating somebody up after a bad defeat isn't journalism, it's bullying. Some situations demand the firm approach – like the Hoddle interview – but others deserve a softer, more human understanding, and it's knowing when and where to apply either that makes you a decent reporter.

What made the situation even worse with Danny is that he's such a decent guy, somebody who would much rather do you a good turn than a bad one. It gnawed away at me and I knew I had to apologize for my conduct. To his absolute credit, there were no hard feelings. He accepted my apology and that I was doing my job, even though I confessed to him I had done it particularly badly on that occasion.

Looking back at all three interviews many years later is interesting. Although time may have passed, the memory of just how awful I felt in the immediate aftermath is as raw today as it was then. They still sting. I regret my handling of all three and it would be very easy to try and banish from my memory, never think about them again, but they were significant learning curves in my career. You have to learn important lessons from moments like these, chiefly to try and not repeat those mistakes again.

7

Career-Threatening Injury

Steven Gerrard is standing talking to me no more than two feet away and I cannot comprehend a single word he's saying. There's a producer from a studio in London giving me instructions via my earpiece but all I have is white noise in both ears. I am broken, terrified, and wracked by an inability to cope with a job that I love with a passion but which is now tearing me apart.

I'm dead behind the eyes, operating on autopilot. We're in the locker room of the Home Depot Centre, home of LA Galaxy, and Stevie could be giving me a sensational line or quote and it wouldn't register. All I can see is his lips moving and when they stop moving, I ask another question. That's the total extent of my interaction.

Fear and fatigue are destroying me mentally. I have reached that stage where I want somebody to take me to one side and say, 'Geoff, you've had a good run but it's time for you to go.' To bring an end to the turmoil, to give me a chance to regroup and recover because – one thing is for certain – I can't go on like this.

How had it got to this? How had my life crumbled to such an extent that I'd had serious discussions with my wife about quitting Sky, selling our house and starting over? How had my mental health deteriorated to the point where I only recognized myself as a robotic shell?

The decline may have been gradual but I knew this was rock bottom.

Looking back now, with the benefit of having worked with some incredible people, I can trace it to something seemingly innocuous, a run-of-the-mill event that should barely have registered as a flicker.

I had a minor medical issue, not much more than a sphincter procedure. The few friends I told about it joked that it had become worn because I spoke out of it so much. A little embarrassing but nothing major. Into hospital, have a very minor op on my back passage and then back home the same day. A few days recuperating and I'd be fine. Or at least, so I thought.

It wasn't until a week or ten days later that I began to suspect something was wrong. I just didn't feel right. It felt like there was something – I don't know – 'stirring' back there. I felt uncomfortable, a bit of an ache, a few below par, but nothing so dramatic that I couldn't put it down to the healing process. It was just . . . odd.

On this particular day in 2015, I had a couple of meetings at Sky's headquarters in Isleworth and, as I was walking into the building, there was a feeling, not like breaking wind or a bowel movement, but just as if something had passed. I headed straight to a toilet cubicle, took off my jeans, and there was bright red blood everywhere.

This can't be good.

I clean myself and the cubicle up using paper towels and toilet paper. Luckily, I was wearing dark jeans, so nothing showed too badly on the outside, but I still had two meetings to get through. Adjusting the handle on my satchel so that it covered my backside (thankfully it was a big one that Phil Neville bought me for my fiftieth birthday; I've told him he saved my arse!), I somehow made it out of the toilet, got through the meetings and escaped from Sky as quickly as I possibly could.

On the hour or so journey home to St Albans, I phoned my surgeon, Richard Cohen, and gave him the low-down. The fact that it was bright red blood was positive, apparently, because darker blood would suggest some-thing far more sinister. More likely, it was an abscess that had developed from an infection, which is nasty but not anywhere near as disturbing from a medical viewpoint.

Apparently, the tell-tale signs of an abscess are flu-like symptoms, chills, cold sweats, a fever; even on the drive home I could feel them developing. My wife, Di, and our three children were away in Norfolk and I was due to meet them there the next day for a week's holiday, so there was nothing I could do but get home.

In these kinds of situations my first call is often to Alan Smith's wife, Penny. Alan and Penny have been our close friends for thirty years, with us each being godparents to each other's children. We have shared so many good times before either couple was married – births of children and other celebrations, as well as the more difficult moments that life inevitably throws at you.

Smudge has never changed in all the time I've known him. Winning the league twice with Arsenal, playing for England, or scoring the winning goal in the Cup Winners' Cup final, he has remained the same down-to-earth, straight-up guy I trust and rely upon. In the absence of Di and, at my wits' end, I called them.

By the time they got to the house, I was in a desperate state, shivering and sweating, with so much blood coming out of me that I'm really worried. Pen took command as usual, ordering Smudge to run me a bath, and I was able to clean myself up a bit. Having taken my temperature and administered paracetamol, they got me to bed while Di was making plans to immediately get back from Norfolk with the kids. Without Smudge and Pen, I'm not sure what I would have done.

From there, everything went on fast forward. The next morning I was taken back into the Princess Grace Hospital in London, where Mr Cohen immediately operated. Not to be too graphic, it was horrendous. The abscess had burst and was oozing not only blood but poison. It meant making an incision and draining the whole area to clean it out as much as possible.

The recuperation process is arguably worse because the wound and the immediate area has to be kept sterile. Easier when it's an external site, so much more difficult when it's internal and exacerbated by the fact that this particular area is so much more likely to become reinfected every time you open your bowels. For eight days in hospital, I had to have the wound cleaned and drained several times a day. It was obviously degrading, but I was so far out of it on a cocktail of drugs that it was like an out-of-body experience.

The pain was, at times, excruciating. Initially, I was hooked up to a morphine drip, had stitches in the wound and a catheter inserted to take away any stale urine which could cause another infection. So I was basically immobile, simply out of it, except for the three or four times a day when the nurses came in to clean me and change my dressing. I honestly don't remember too much from the first couple of days, but I could see how worried Di and the family were to see me with so many tubes coming in and out of me.

There comes a time when the doctors have to start weaning you off the morphine because of the dangers of opiate addiction, and that's when the pain really starts to kick in. I didn't know what to do with myself; it was agony at times. The nurses want to get you up and active, but that brings its own problems because movement causes bleeding. There would be moments when I was shuffling down a corridor with a walking frame and I'd look behind me and there would be a trails of blood splatters, so a poor nurse has to clean me up, get me back to bed and you're back at square one again.

I have to pay tribute to Di at this stage because she was incredible. We've been together over thirty years, but I know she didn't sign up for what she had to go through with me for those weeks after I left the Princess Grace. Basically, she set up a field hospital at our house. She decamped to the spare room as she knew that I would be awake at all hours, put plastic sheeting down to make a pathway to the toilet and set up a bedside table with all the medication.

I've kept the chart which told Di when I had to be medicated and how much. It's like a glossary of pain relief . . . Metronidazole, Oxycodeine, Oxycontin, Pregabalin, Cefuroxime. I rattled when I walked – or when I was actually able to take a few stuttering steps without blood spattering the plastic sheeting every step of the way.

The worst thing was Di having to clean me and treat the wound as best she could. It got to the stage where I was wearing adult incontinence pants to mop up the blood and God alone knows how Di coped, especially in those early days. I was like an infant, unable to take care of myself or control the bleeding or the pain, totally reliant on her to look after me, hour after hour, day after day. It took half an hour just to get to the bathroom, have a shower and clean me up, and we're talking four or five times a day. I still struggle to put into words the depth of her patience, resilience and kindness. Truth be told, anyone who is lucky enough to know Di will tell you that those are the hallmarks of her character.

Looking back, I think it was after the first few weeks that the problems began to set in mentally. The pain was beginning to ease but I was still so weak and fatigued that I could barely lift a leg. I wasn't bed-bound any more, but it was all I could do to make it down the stairs into my office, where I'd crash on a sofa and lie there watching television in between sleeping. I was living in a fog that I couldn't begin to shake off, even as I became physically stronger.

Work was obviously impossible but I didn't really tell

Sky the whole story. If you break your leg, people ask you how you did it, how long it will take to recover and all that. When you tell people you've had an operation on your arse, it shuts the conversation down pretty quickly, trust me! I couldn't hide what I was going through from my family or close friends, but to the outside world I was pretty jocular, tried to make light of it yet all the time knowing I still struggled to walk ten yards or more.

The fact was, I wasn't making enough progress physically and that was affecting my mental state. To compound the situation, I could feel another growth developing in my back passage and I was at my wits' end as to what it could mean. So another trip back to hospital, another exploratory operation to discover I'd now developed a fistula on my sphincter, a growth caused by an impacted hair growing the wrong way and burrowing itself into my flesh and becoming infected. It was like going into hospital for pneumonia and finding out, just for good measure, you'd caught measles too. Another four days in the Princess Grace.

So that's two operations down, still in terrible pain but knowing physically I was going to recover, I thought a by-product of the recovery was the chronic fatigue I was suffering, the inability to raise myself for more than an hour or so before I needed to sleep again. I just wasn't able to function in any meaningful way. I felt I was just drifting through days, listless, with no interest in very much at all. About the only thing I could do was watch television, and I ploughed through the whole boxset of *House of Cards* in a week, slumped on the sofa in my office.

Those closest to me knew there was something wrong more quickly than I did, but we thought it was just a symptom of coming off high-dosage and strong opiates. Di and the kids saw a normally outgoing and ebullient husband and father shrink, while my parents, John and Jean, saw a deterioration in my mental state that made me almost unrecognizable. The only way I can describe it is as a permanent fog that I knew I had to battle through but wasn't able to see any clear path out of. There was simply no fuel in the tank.

I tried, I really tried, as much for the sake of the family as myself. We'd make plans to go out and visit friends or for a family trip and, honestly, I'd be out the door and to the car when Di would look over at me, see that I wasn't right or ready for this, and protect me by telling the kids that I needed a bit more rest and that it would be better for them to go without me. Then it would be back to bed or the sofa. That happened countless times.

When I think back, I remember one of the nurses at the Princess Grace telling me I should ready myself for depression, which took me completely by surprise. I asked why, because I felt I was mentally strong and able to cope with pretty much anything. He just pointed out that I'd been through a hell of a lot, that I'd been in a bad way and that my body had to find a way to cope. To be honest, I just completely dismissed it. He was just being a do-gooder, too caring, trying to baby me and wrap me in swaddling cloth. At the time I thought it a daft and inappropriate thing to say. In hindsight I'm embarrassed at my reaction.

That was my summer, drifting along, thinking it was merely a symptom of my recovery but knowing deep down there was something desperately wrong, yet it was nothing

I could pin down or name. My target for a return to work was 8 August, the first game of the new season, and I got there. That, though, was a huge mistake, because I was ignoring my body, ignoring my mind and simply trying to put a brave face on it.

The reasons were two-fold. Firstly, the wound had healed, I could get around fine, so there was no reason not to be back at work. Secondly, I was afraid to say to Sky I was having problems, even though it was obvious I was struggling. I'd be interviewing a player post-match and he'd say something and then a couple of questions later, I'd ask him about something he'd already answered a minute or so earlier. I was missing so much because I wasn't able to focus, which is a massive handicap when you're live or even pre-recorded. That's when the terror and panic sets in.

But as the season started, frankly I was terrified because, in the job I do, you cannot survive if you're off the pace; it catches up with you so quickly. I was petrified that people would be saying, 'He's not what he was' or 'He's lost it', and that would be the end. So, I was hiding, covering up, trying not to let people see any weakness or shortcomings, and driving myself on even though I knew I was lost.

For example, if I had to drive up to Manchester for a game, I'd book a hotel for an overnight stay but ensure I could get an early check-in. Then I'd drive north as far as Birmingham, drinking can after can of Red Bull and eating chocolate for some kind of energy just to get through the journey. Perhaps I'd drive for an hour but then have to stop off at a service station on the way, wind my car seat back and sleep for an hour before getting back on the road. As soon as I got to the hotel, I'd immediately go to bed for another couple of hours because I was exhausted, wiped out.

Then it was a case of getting through the game as best as I could, fuelled by coffee and Mars bars but knowing everything was blurred around the edges and I'd lost all my sharpness. Surely other people could see it, because I recognized it in myself. I was at a total loss. I was zombified even though my mood wasn't particularly low. What I didn't understand then is that depression has nothing to do with being happy or sad. There was no black cloud hanging over me; I was just a muted version of myself, not wanting to socialize. I shunned people, especially work colleagues, because I didn't want to show any weakness.

Di held the fort magnificently. Over the years, I've often been away for five or six weeks at a time during tournaments, when she's had to look after the house, the children, Dennis the dog, everything. But this was like being at home physically but mentally completely absent.

As ever, I have to say that people in football were incredible. So many times they've rallied around and helped me out, including Gary Lewin, the former Arsenal and England physio, and somebody who has been a good friend for decades. England were training at The Grove hotel near Watford, and I went to see him because I just thought there was still something physically wrong with me.

I told him I was struggling and, even though he couldn't do a full work-out on me, he did some tests and gave me some super-vitamins to try and at least give me some kind of boost. But he told me I had to go and see my surgeon or explore other routes to find the cause. This will not go away, he said ominously.

So why did I then put myself through a trip to Los Angeles when it was clear I should have been about as far away from California as it was humanly possible to be? Call it a bit of professional vanity, if you like. Stevie G and Frank Lampard, who was playing for New York City against the Galaxy, were strong contacts of mine. If there was a piece to be done with either, then it would usually have been down to me to set it up and carry it through. Plus Sky didn't know there was anything wrong with me at this time. I'd done my best to keep it hidden.

Many years later, after I had spoken publicly about my mental health challenges, our managing director at the time, Barney Francis, said he wished Sky had done more to help me. Truth be told, they couldn't help because I didn't feel comfortable in telling them. Thankfully, the understanding of mental health in the workplace has become far more widespread, and I would have no qualms now whatsoever in telling my employer if I was struggling.

When I flew out, I was very fortunate to be accompanied by one of my favourite cameramen, a great guy by the name of Scott Drummond, a former heavyweight boxer and an absolute man-mountain. I confided in him that I was struggling and he simply said, 'Don't worry, I'll look after you.' Which he did. But he knew instinctively something more was up. Even though I told him I was struggling, I was still trying to cover things up, trying my hardest not to give too much away. Normally, I'd be helping him out, carrying some of his kit, lights, tripods and so on, but on this trip I was utterly exhausted. It was all I could do to carry myself, let alone any kit.

Leading up to the interview with Stevie in the Galaxy locker room, I was terrified. Looking back on the video, I'm dead behind the eyes, there's nothing there. My delivery is robotic; I'm no more than a shell. My mind was racing, fixated on the list of questions I'd memorized.

All I'm doing is looking at his mouth to see when he stopped speaking so I could ask the next question. Had he finished with a question of his own or asked me something, I'd have been dead in the water because nothing, simply nothing, was going in.

If Stevie had said, 'That's it, I'm jacking this America lark in and going back to my wife and kids in Liverpool,' I wouldn't have had a clue. Nothing was registering. The sound wasn't mute, I could hear him, but nothing was going in. My producer back in London was talking through my earpiece but I'm struggling to comprehend one person standing in front of me, let alone hear someone else in my ear.

I'm like a wobbly shelf. If there's one thing on it, I can just about cope. Put something else alongside it and I'm all over the place.

I came back from the States shaken to the core. I identify that moment as the one where I knew the game was up and that I had really serious problems that I needed to get sorted. I'd only been away three or four days, but when I got home Di was shocked and upset to see the state I was in. She'd had her reservations about me going back to work in the first place, whereas I was just hoping beyond hope I'd wake up one morning and snap out of it.

Alan Curbishley, somebody else I've been fortunate enough to call a friend for many, many years, was also concerned when I bumped into him. I knew I could trust him so when he asked how I was feeling, I just laid it out, told him I was having a desperate time and nothing was getting better. 'Curbs' was helping out at Fulham at the time, and the club had been fortunate that when Jean Tigana was manager, he insisted that the very best, state-of-the-art medical facilities were installed at their Motspur Park training ground.

I went down and Dr Mark Taylor saw me and ran all sorts of tests, which he sent off to the United States for the results. But when they came back, they couldn't find anything physically wrong or untoward. That really just reinforced my feelings of despair. Far from being a waste of time, though, the hand of fate intervened that day and led me to my ultimate salvation.

It was while I was at the Fulham training ground that I got into a conversation with Sarah Brookes, the former director of communications and somebody I'd known for many years, having shared many a laugh/glass of wine with her. This time, though, it was a serious chat. We were sitting in the players' canteen having coffee when we were joined by Scott Parker, who listened to what I was saying, how I described my feelings and the sense of helplessness that had come over me.

He waited a couple of minutes for me to finish and then asked, 'Have you ever considered some psychological help, too, maybe seeing a psychiatrist?' By this stage in his career, Scott had been at a number of clubs and psychological assistance was becoming more common within football clubs. That hadn't even crossed my mind, though.

If he'd have said, 'Have you thought about witchcraft to cure you?' I wouldn't have been more surprised and taken aback. It was *never* something I'd even thought about, not in a million years; it was a completely alien concept. But the more Scott talked about it, the more he opened my eyes.

To be honest, if somebody had told me I should dance naked round a maypole at midnight with an orange on my head and that it would help, then I would have done it because I was that desperate. I was trying to physically find a way out, exploring so many avenues and yet nothing was working. As Curbs said to me, 'You know you want to go north but you can't decide whether to take the M1, the A1, A40, get the train or a plane. You know where you are is in the wrong place, you know you have to get somewhere else, you're just unsure how to get there.'

It was only through the care and generosity of Curbs that I went to Fulham, had the chance meeting with Sarah and Scott which, basically, gave me back my life. I needed something so desperately at that time because I had all my emotions on the surface; I constantly found myself in tears or on the brink of tears. It was an intolerable situation, a dam that needed to burst.

So there's something new to explore now, another option. The next step is who do I see? Like everybody, I go with the people whose opinions I trust and to a man they all championed: Dr Steve Peters. I'd been aware of his work and his renowned book, *The Chimp Paradox*, and the fact it had been hailed as a ground-breaking book on the subject. He was also working with elite sportsmen at Liverpool FC, with the FA and the Great Britain cycling team. Basically, he was *the* man.

But that success meant it was also almost impossible to get an appointment with him, especially as a potential new patient referral. That's again where the generosity of the football and media business came into play. Steven Gerrard had worked with him at Liverpool and a true friend, Matt Lawton of *The Times*, knew Dr Peters from covering cycling. Both of them reached out on my behalf, explaining that I needed some help. I know how fortunate I am to have people like that in my life.

My first meeting with Dr Peters was in Manchester, where I was covering Manchester City v Juventus in the Champions League. He came to my room in the Radisson and I've rarely been so nervous, more from fears of him not being able to help me than of surrendering myself in the way he required or being honest about my scenario. I was simply petrified he was going to say he couldn't help me, or that what I was suffering wasn't a psychological thing.

I was so desperate because my existence was really a non-existence. I'd already talked to Di and my parents about the possibility of having to pack in work, selling the house and trying to find a new, less demanding way of life. That was 100 per cent looking like the most likely outcome, because there was no way I could carry on like this.

I've always prided myself on being mentally agile, light on my feet. I can respond, operate off the cuff if needed; I can improvise and ad-lib. But every tool I needed to do the job had been stripped from me, and I was frightened of telling Sky in case they took me off the job. Even if I had a rest period and came back, they might say, 'Not as good as he was.' It was a perfect storm and it horrified me.

All this was rushing through my mind when Dr Peters walked into my room that day. Immediately, though, he took control of the room which, until you meet Steve, seems the opposite of his persona. He's the most genteel, relatively softly spoken man you could wish to meet, yet his aura is incredible. He has the ability to cut straight to the heart of the problem.

In my job, I think I have a small insight into psychology and an amateur reading of body language as I try to gauge a person's mood and understand the signs before I speak to them. So, I sat down in front of Steve with my arms folded – and I knew he'd probably pick up on that. Before he spoke, I said, 'I've got my arms folded because I've not done any real exercise for eight or nine months, my shirt's slightly too tight and gaping a bit so I'm trying to cover that up.'

His response was delivered like a right hook swiftly followed by an uppercut. 'Defensive pose? Bad start. Justification? Even worse.' *Wow!* He got my attention like he'd thrown a bucket of ice water in my face.

From that moment, I spare no details. I tell him everything I've been through, all my struggles, how my mind is racing, my inability to concentrate, the constant fear and panic as I plough through a fog that has a never-ending electric storm at its centre, all exacerbated by being live on television.

He listened, asked all the pertinent questions, nodded and then sat back. 'Right,' he said, 'I know why you're feeling like you are.' This is it, I thought! I am going to hear from the very lips of the most respected guru in this particular business. After months of pain, suffering, constant anxiety and moments when I've even questioned my own sanity, I'm going to get an answer to all my problems. Slowly and thoughtfully he said, 'I can tell you why you're not well, it's because you're not well.'

You what? Is he taking the piss? All that build-up and that's his highly educated conclusion based on years of experience? I thought he was joking at first. Is that really all he's got? Well basically yes, therein lies his genius. He could clearly see I was underwhelmed by his synopsis when he gave me the following analogy. 'You interview footballers, don't you? If you went to see one today who had a broken leg, you would ask questions such as, How long will you be out for? When do you expect the cast to come off and when will you be able to jog again?' I nodded. 'Would you ask him why he wasn't in the team and scoring goals?' I got it in an instant.

He told me I'd had three major assaults on my body and my body has not physically recovered, yet I refused to accept that was the case. My body was in flight-or-fight mode because I wasn't ready to accept the ramifications of the operations I'd had and I wasn't managing them accordingly.

He felt I was suffering from depression, which manifested itself in chronic fatigue, and everything else stemmed from that. Of course he was right. Part of me felt foolish that I hadn't even considered that, whether it was from egotism or a macho attitude that I had refused to countenance the possibility was that simple.

Dr Peters made it clear there was going to be no straight line to recovery. If tomorrow I felt knackered, instead of fighting it and thinking, 'Oh no, here's the same symptoms again', simply go to bed for a couple of hours. So what? Who cares? The body needs to rest and recover; it doesn't need my mind to fight it and try covering everything up. Acceptance was the absolute key.

He said there and then in my hotel room that from the initial operation, it would be two years before I was feeling completely myself again, but that it would get a lot better a lot more quickly. Looking back, he was right almost to the day. It was astonishing.

A little while later, I told my dad that I was struggling and I had to go and see Steve. My dad phoned the next day to ask how I was and what is it that Steve says to give you such a lift? The best way I could describe it was the old Alan Sherman song, 'Camp Grenada', where the kid is continually moaning about everything and asking his parents to take him home, then the sun comes out and all is well with the world once more.

Steve has the ability to lift the gloom, lift the clouds, dissect the uncertainty. It meant that by the New Year I was able to function so much more capably at work, and by spring I felt in control and understood all the coping functions and mechanisms I had to employ, which was a huge step forward. I took anti-depressants for quite a long time, and to be honest I found it difficult to come off them several times, but by the middle of 2020, I'd kicked them completely.

I'm lucky there have been no setbacks or relapses, and now I feel I'm evangelical about mental health. I was hosting *The Debate* show on Sky where the panel was Chris Kirkland and Kris Boyd, and we started talking about mental health and I felt completely relaxed in talking about my own circumstances and what I'd been through. Whereas at the time there was shame involved and a deliberate decision to try and cover things up, now I knew I could be open and honest about my situation. That felt a hugely positive step.

I've also encouraged players and former players, people I know and who trust me, to seek help if they ever feel they have any signs of a mental struggle. Football is so much more accepting than it was even four or five years ago, and I think most businesses are the same. If this was now, I would have no qualms in telling Sky what I was going through and them being understanding in being able to take proper time off to cope.

There's no question it has made me more aware and accepting of my own fragility and also other people's. I can't say I'm glad it happened because of the effect it had on the people around me – on Di, my children, as well as my parents – but I'm not sure I'm sorry it happened because of what it taught me about myself and mental health.

But to have potentially lost my job at Sky would have been devastating. For almost thirty years, I'd been on the touchline, privileged to work in a game I love, building relationships with people I admire, witnessing a world so very few fans in the ground or at home ever even glimpse. Not for the first time in my life, I would say I'm a very lucky boy.

8

Managing Managers

It was Gordon Strachan who said managers go through ecstasy or hell for ninety minutes. Afterwards, they want to tell the world how brilliantly their team has done, or just slide away to reflect on the pain of defeat. Then they come out of the dressing room and there's Geoff Shreeves waiting at the end of the corridor like the Grim Reaper and the microphone in his hand may as well be the scythe of doom.

Bit harsh!

I have always had the utmost regard for managers and the fact they are very often the only people who ever have to front up for their football clubs. Of course, they're answerable for results and performances – that's part of the remit – and they expect to be either praised or criticized for the way their team has played. I've got no problem with asking the questions they don't particularly want to answer in that respect.

What doesn't sit well with me is when a manager is cast adrift, when they're answering questions that are nothing to do with their jobs, but they're sent out by chairman and chief executives who are content to hide away, knowing somebody else is taking the flak for them. For example, when Roman Abramovich put Chelsea up for sale, why was it that Thomas Tuchel was the *only* person at the club forced to face the media and get inundated with questions outside of his remit? What does a manager know about geopolitics and the war in Ukraine?

More to the point, where were any members of the Chelsea board when the storm was at its height? For me it's just plain wrong that Tuchel was forced into that position, unable to truly give the answers the media demanded and yet the hierarchy at Stamford Bridge stayed silent. Now they may well say there were legal reasons why they couldn't speak, and I want to be clear that this is purely an example as Chelsea are far from alone in this; it happens all the time.

At the time of writing, there have been 433 managers at the fifty different clubs who have played in the Premier League, and I think I've interviewed well over 400 of them. There must have been a few caretakers or interim bosses who slipped through the net, but not too many. There have been a few who I'd be content if I never saw again, but the vast majority I like and admire. How can you not have empathy for a person who takes a job, knowing that it's going to end in the sack but that, along the way, there will be moments of exhilarating highs and devastating lows? To actually volunteer for that makes you a special kind of person.

More than that, their every word and move is chronicled, studied and forensically dissected. They are scrutinized as much as any world leader or politician, their decisions questioned at every turn, and they become the lightning rods for abuse. The pressure is immense and all-consuming, and they have to live with the brutality of the job every day of their lives. It can do terrible things to good men.

Ole Gunnar Solskjaer was a joy to work with when he was Manchester United manager. His personality didn't change, he was always unfailingly polite and understanding that I had a job to do when they'd been beaten, and he accepted the scrutiny of those questions. After United's last televised game in the 2020–1 season, I thanked him for all his help and wished him the best in the Europa League final the following week. We shook hands and he said, 'I appreciate that and thanks for everything this season.'

That's why, when things reach their lowest ebb for a manager, it's almost too painful to be around them. Those last few games for Ole, when they had been beaten up by Liverpool and Manchester City and we'd all lost count of the number of times Harry Maguire or Bruno Fernandes had come out and apologized for the team's performances, were horrific. Yet even then Ole maintained such an air of dignity that my overriding feeling was one of admiration rather than pity.

At the end, when they'd been beaten so badly by Watford, he was still bright and cheery, smiling his way through our interview, putting on the kind of brave face he'd had to perfect over the weeks. Something didn't tally with me, all this talk of it not being 'goodbye' yet, made no sense.

Sometimes the simplest questions can be the most informative, so I asked, 'How low do you feel right now?' And, horribly, he just crumpled in front of my eyes, as if the air had been sucked out of his body and he slumped with the realization this would probably be his last game in charge of Manchester United.

There is no satisfaction in that scenario; it is merely another part of the job that has to be done professionally and with integrity. Hammering a manager when he's obviously at his lowest ebb is never good television. It makes you look like a bully or some soulless ghoul, intent only on beating somebody into submission – and I've learnt from bitter experience that is never a good look.

Honesty is the only way to approach these kinds of situations because friendship sometimes has to take a back seat, even with somebody you've built a relationship with over many years. I first interviewed Arsène Wenger when he joined Arsenal in 1996 and, even at a conservative estimate, we'd speak thirty times a season. Now multiply that by the twenty-two years he was in charge and there is obviously going to be a rapport and understanding of each other's role. I know what makes him tick, he knows how I work; it's a relationship based on that kind of mutual respect.

Not that that prevents moments when the relationship spills over into outright antagonism. After Arsenal had been beaten 8-2 by Manchester United at Old Trafford in 2011, there was no room for soft-soap questions, not after that kind of humiliation. In fact, for the first time in the club's history, Arsenal compensated their travelling fans with free tickets. Arsène had played a weakened team;

they were thrashed out of sight and Wenger had to face an inquisition.

One of the first questions I asked was would he resign on the basis of that performance and defeat? No, Wenger would not be walking away. That then begs the question: do you think the board will back you? Those are brutal questions, but I know that if I don't ask them, they were guaranteed to be asked in Wenger's subsequent press conference.

My questions were direct, and I could see the anger building in his eyes which, for somebody who prides himself in putting all emotion aside in interviews, was telling. After the interview was over, I thought it probably made sense to speak to Arsène and talk through what had just gone on, but I couldn't catch his eye. In fact, it felt like he was going out of his way not to engage.

After he'd retreated to the dressing room, Arsenal's head of media, Mark Gonella, emerged and we started chatting. I told him I'd like to chat things through with Arsène because, obviously, we had a rapport and I didn't want anything to jeopardize that. 'Geoff, he's not in the mood for that. In fact, I've never seen him like that before,' Mark said. 'The boss has just told me he wanted to hit you during that interview, he was so angry.'

Now whether that was over my line of questioning or just the fact his side had been destroyed at the home of their greatest rivals, I wasn't sure. Certainly, losing as badly at the hands of Sir Alex Ferguson would have done nothing for Wenger's mood, but I just think there was something in that match that was pivotal for Arsenal, a sense they could no longer truly compete. Years later, I had lunch with Arsène, and he admitted he'd played a weakened team after a hugely draining Champions League fixture. He expected to lose but never as badly as shipping eight, so his post-match anger was understandable. 'Geoff, I wanted to hit you that day, it's true,' he said, 'but you were not the only one that day – there were many others.'

Wenger was always fascinating, and I probably spent more time with him than any other manager throughout my career, given that my home in St Albans was just minutes from the training ground and I was always the man on the spot when Sky needed an interview. From the first time I met him, he was different and unlike any manager that I'd encountered. For one thing, he never ducked an interview, never made an excuse or stepped away. He would always front up and answer questions without resorting to platitudes.

I know he found me tricky in those early days because I was young and hungry, and this was an opportunity for me to speak to one of the most interesting people ever to enter English football. I'd built a great relationship with a lot of the Arsenal players at the time, some of whom, like Tony Adams, Lee Dixon and Steve Bould, I'd known since they joined the club, so I was hearing about the revolution taking place and the new methods the manager was employing.

There were vastly experienced pros who had won things under George Graham, both domestically and in Europe, and who had enjoyed a level of success only a very few could match. Now they were being told to largely forget everything that had gone before, because the first foreign manager in the Premier League was implementing new training methods, new diets, new fitness demands and a complete reinvention of everything to do with the club.

It was a question I put to Ray Parlour on stage at a Legends of Football dinner in honour of Arsène. How were a group of hard-bitten and cynical players, many of whom had been members of the infamous Tuesday Drinking Club, convinced to abandon half a lifetime of habits in favour of this manager's methodology?

'Easy one to answer, that,' Parlour replied. 'He doubled our money!'

What Wenger brought to his dealings with the media was a level of insight most of us had never experienced. Unlike so many of his colleagues at the time, he was happy to sit down and talk about tactics, formations, and the psychology behind his thinking. Too many other managers seemed afraid to open up on that front, preferring not to show their hands, as if they would be revealing some kind of state secret if they talked.

For that, Wenger was scrutinized more than any other manager. Was it a reaction to a foreign manager coming in and showing the English game just how far behind the times it was? Probably. But speaking to him now that he's no longer a club manager, he believes that managers today have a far easier ride than he did when he first arrived and that the media – both broadcast and print – is a lot more forgiving of the reasons for failure trotted out by some modern managers.

He's possibly right, but I also believe that goes back to the time when Wenger first arrived and he was taking on Ferguson in a way that nobody had before. Yes, Blackburn had won the title thanks to Jack Walker's investment, Kenny Dalglish's shrewd management and Alan Shearer's goals, but Arsenal were an existential threat to Ferguson and United's dominance; here was a team that could out-play the opposition but also out-fight them if necessary – and it was the kind of challenge Ferguson had never faced.

Being in the tunnel for matches between United and Arsenal was an experience I have never forgotten. Such was the competitive nature of both squads there was an intense dislike between the two managers and between the two sets of players, that's probably the only description that fits. It was visceral and the tension was palpable; the air crackled because they knew that one mistake or one moment of brilliance would be the deciding factor.

Ferguson was strategic, building up an agenda with the media even weeks before games against Arsenal. But Wenger was his match, albeit in a slightly more discreet way, happy to pull the pin from a grenade and roll it towards Old Trafford with the odd phrase or barbed comment. Never have I met two men more unalike in character but identical in their drive and passion for success.

What I liked about Arsène – and what I still admire – is his honesty. Ask him a straight question and you got a straight answer. I understand why he thinks I was tricky in those early days because I realized that I could throw everything at him, and he would answer unflinchingly. Come at him from a different angle with your questions and he'd be prepared. He was never off-balance or content to throw up a cheap answer; it was always considered.

There was also a warmth to him privately that didn't come across on screen. I remember arriving at the training ground for an interview one day, feeling out of sorts and obviously appearing somewhat shabby.

'Geoff, you look like shit. Is there a problem?' was Arsène's opening salvo.

I explained that over the course of the previous night, our three kids had, all at different times, joined Di and me in bed, and that I was absolutely knackered having had barely a minute's kip – that was the problem.

He said, 'No, Geoff, one day your children will be older, and they will no longer need to come to the bed because they don't need you any more. That is a bigger problem.'

For a man who actually admitted to me he had learnt to remove emotion from his work life, it was an incredibly touching moment, because I know how much he sacrificed with his family in his devotion and obsession with football.

There was also a humour about Wenger that was only rarely glimpsed on camera or in press conferences. The Sky cameras were at Wigan when Roberto Martinez was in charge and, after the game, he invited me and the floor manager, John Smart, into his office for a drink.

That is one of the great privileges of the job, often being invited to sit with the managers after a game as they dissect the match, admit where they made mistakes and generally gossip about chairmen, directors, chief executives and players. Wenger would very rarely meet up post-match but, on this occasion, he and his assistant Pat Rice came in for a glass of wine.

As ever, the conversation got on to players. Pat was talking dismissively of Nicklas Bendtner who, yet again, had failed to live up to his potential but who carried about him an air of arrogance. 'The problem with Bendtner is that he thinks he's the best player at this club,' Pat said, which got a bit of a laugh.

Suddenly, Wenger cut him off with a sharp, 'You're wrong, Pat.' It was a bit embarrassing, a manager talking to his assistant in that tone in front of us all, especially somebody as experienced and admired as Pat who, we could see, was a bit taken aback. Inwardly, I cringed.

'The problem with Bendtner is not that he thinks he's the best player at Arsenal,' Wenger continued. 'It's that he thinks he's the best player in the world. That's his problem.'

Suddenly the room was in stitches, Pat laughing the loudest, and I wondered to myself why Arsène didn't do this sort of thing more often and enjoy the camaraderie between managers who, just for a moment, could relax, before facing another week of pressure back on the training pitch, preparing for the next ninety minutes of anguish.

My greatest wish is that Wenger could have gone out at Arsenal in different circumstances. There was no joy in that last season, with so many fans calling for his head, despite this being the man who had transformed not just a football club but the whole culture of our game. Rarely do I feel uncomfortable with any line of questioning, but having to ask a man who had given so much to football whether his race was run was painful and, in a way, I was relieved when he decided to step down.

Now, when we meet up, it's no longer football, football, football. He likes to talk about politics and religion and art and it's obvious he is doing everything possible to enjoy life away from the game. Mind you, if you ever get the chance to visit him at home, take your own teabags and milk because he never has anything in the cupboards or fridge.

Wenger and Ferguson used to be the ultimate

manipulators of the media, but now more managers realize the power of a TV camera and how their words will resonate. The problem for us is that we are always their first port of call when emotions are still running so high, which leads to sometimes unnecessary confrontations.

For me, that's part of the contract. If Sky want the managers in their moment of glory and excitement when they've won a match, a cup, or a title, then we have to accept that we might also get a manager at his worst. If that leads to awkwardness and discomfort, so be it.

I have officially lost count of the times when interviews have been combative to the point of aggression, albeit thankfully never physical. There's not a manager who hasn't taken umbrage with a question and not a manager who hasn't sounded off unreasonably, either when the cameras have been rolling or in the privacy of the tunnel or touchline.

The important thing is to never take it personally. So last season, when David Moyes was particularly hostile after West Ham had lost to Arsenal in a vital match in terms of Champions League qualification, I accepted he was furious with several refereeing decisions and was venting at the first opportunity given to him. Equally, I wasn't about to just sit back and take it. You stand your corner sensibly and tactfully, pointing out incidents that might not have registered with him during the game or give him the other side of the argument.

I watched the subsequent press conferences with radio and print journalists. Moyes didn't make the same points in those because, I guess, he'd got them off his chest with me. Again, no problem at all, it goes with the territory. We are first up.

I'm not sure why it should be, but there is a sense of fun between managers which is disappearing. The days when every manager would go into their opposition's office after a match are gone. More often now the managers will fulfil their media obligations and be gone, instead of taking time to relax just for a moment. Which is a real shame.

I don't think it's purely because of the numbers of foreign managers in the Premier League, although it does seem to be a ritual unique to the British game, because the likes of José Mourinho saw the value in meeting up after a game for a glass of wine or a beer and chance to decompress. In fact, Mourinho embraced everything to do with the English game and, in particular, the media.

For Sky, he was an absolute dream. I'd got to know him through our Champions League coverage, this young, charismatic and handsome presence at Porto who was shaking up the establishment, ruffling feathers along the way and using the media to his advantage at every opportunity. Want to do a piece strolling around the training ground? Sure, come over whenever you like. Want to spend some time in the build-up to a big European game? Not a problem, take all the time you need.

It was the same when he arrived at Chelsea in 2004. He knew the value of a television interview, what he wanted from it, and what he could achieve in terms of his messaging and his profile, not always in that order. He reached out to us and made it perfectly clear he was happy to help.

When Chelsea clinched their first Premier League title at the Reebok Stadium in Bolton, I was stood next to the bench and the first call he made was to his wife back in Portugal and then – even before he joined his jubilant players, and Roman Abramovich, who had joined them on the pitch – he gave Sky an interview that will live long in my memory for its overwhelming sense of joy and achievement. Sometimes, it's not just the words but also the occasion that makes for good television.

I know he could rub people up the wrong way, but he was just a magnet for the cameras, with his brash persona, his uppity stance, his poking and prodding of the opposition and referees; it was gold dust for us. As he was taking the Premier League by storm in that first season, we heard that the BBC were preparing a documentary on him and giving it the full works: high production values and a budget to go around the world getting all the footage they needed.

It was made very clear to me that Sky would *not* be beaten to the punch on this hurricane that had shaken up the English game. The BBC had been at it for about two months, but I was told I had a cameraman, a fixer and a translator and a week to come up with the goods. No pressure, then.

But it was fantastic, going over to Portugal and retracing José's steps and his career path, although it wasn't exactly plain sailing. We'd tracked down his first university lecturer, who we'd been told had a major influence on Mourinho, opening his eyes to the way teaching impacted on coaching development. Through the translator, I asked whether he recognized the potential in the young Mourinho.

For about two minutes he spoke, with me picking up the odd word like Bobby Charlton, Porto, Champions League, Eusebio, with the rest obviously a detailed analysis of the young Mourinho's character. At the end of the spiel, the translator just looked at me and, with the straightest face, said, 'No, he didn't.' That was the end of her – she was sacked and the fixer took over.

Mourinho didn't want to be involved as he'd already made a commitment to the BBC, but he was happy for us to tell him who we'd interviewed, what importance they'd played in his story and whether there was anybody else we should speak to. He didn't block anybody from speaking to us and he encouraged others who we might not have got, and word reached us that he was very happy with the end result.

That was the side of Mourinho people rarely see amidst all the bravado and supreme self-confidence: the generosity of spirit. He absolutely loves dogs and what they give to a family, so when he heard that our beloved golden retriever, Dennis, had passed, was one of the first to send a consoling text message.

He also knew the rules of engagement where Sky was concerned, even when he was at his lowest ebb following his first sacking by Chelsea. I basically took a crew out to doorstep him back in Portugal, hoping for that first interview. Frankly, we were intruding on his personal space, and he had every right to take umbrage with us. Instead, we met up for a coffee and he explained that, owing to the terms of his contract, he couldn't discuss his dismissal and, while he was happy for us to be there, he wouldn't be giving an interview. Most managers, it has to be said, would have slammed the door in my face or just blanked me. José was just very decent.

He was more than decent when he was Real Madrid manager, and over for a scouting mission at Old Trafford with Manchester United their opponents in the Champions League that midweek. I was covering both games but had to dash back from Manchester to London before a swift turnaround and then out to Spain within twenty-four hours.

We were exchanging text messages and I told him about my travel plans. The next text was simply 'What's your passport number?' A bit confused, I told him, and the next message gave details of the private terminal at Manchester Airport where Real's private jet was parked because he'd swung it for me to travel out to Madrid on the club plane with him – all very relaxed, all very luxurious, I have to say.

He was also extremely self-aware; he knew exactly what people thought of him and played up to that image more often than not. He didn't care how many noses he put out of joint, his only driver was winning, no matter how that was achieved. I remember the night his Inter side lost 1-0 to Barcelona in the semi-final of the Champions League in the Nou Camp but went through on aggregate 3-2. It was a superb tactically disciplined victory, and I said to him away from the cameras, 'Well done, you didn't just park the bus, you parked the fucking plane!' He couldn't contain his laughter!

Despite his abrasive personality, José was actually the only big-name manager I've never crossed swords with, perhaps because he appreciated that understanding between managers and the media better than anybody.

Kenny Dalglish was mischievous. I'd seen him wrong-foot many reporters over the years, tie them up in knots for his own amusement, not because he didn't want to help but because he hated lazy questions and lazy journalism. If you said to Kenny, 'People say Mike Newell is not the ideal striking partner for Alan Shearer.' Or 'People say your Blackburn side isn't as entertaining as Manchester United,' his immediate response would be, 'Which people? Can you name them?' And he was quite right, that's sloppy questioning.

When Blackburn won the title, he was fine with Sky. Not great, not special, but he was OK with us. When I became the reporter, he was then Liverpool manager and I was going to be dealing with him on a regular basis, win, lose or draw. Which was no problem, as long as I was always on my game.

Where we did infamously lock horns was over the Luis Suárez-Patrice Evra racism incident. Suárez had served an eight-game ban for racially abusing Evra and, on only his second match back, was due to go to Old Trafford, where it had been expected he would shake hands with the United defender in the usual pre-match tradition. He didn't and our cameras clearly showed that he didn't.

It was obviously the lead story. There was no avoiding it, and I knew it demanded some answers from the Liverpool manager, but Kenny simply didn't want to go there. Numerous times I asked him about Suárez refusing to shake Evra's hand, but he was just not going to comment despite the seriousness of the situation.

Such was the magnitude of the interview, the BBC got in touch and asked if they could run it on *Match of the Day* and it is the one and only time an interview of mine has run in full on the BBC and they credited both me and Sky.

A day or so later, Dalglish publicly apologized for the fact that he did not conduct himself in a way 'befitting of a Liverpool manager' during the interview.

Thankfully, not everything has to be so tempestuous. In fact, sometimes you play the long game and protect your interview subject as much as possible. I suppose you could argue that's not the mentality of a hard-bitten hack desperate for the story, but when somebody you admire slips up, they deserve the benefit of the doubt.

I'd always had a soft spot for Bobby Robson, dating back to that first World Cup in 1990 where I enjoyed the best four weeks of a fledgling career, following his England side around Italy. Subsequently our paths had crossed when he was a studio guest for international games, and I loved his company and the stories he would tell.

Famously, although he was absolutely as sharp as a tack and one of the brightest football brains around, he was prone to the odd malapropism or mangled syntax. It was an endearing quality, one that his players loved him for and which the media treated kindly.

When it became clear he was favourite to get the Newcastle United job after the sacking of Ruud Gullit, it was a massive story; Bobby Robson coming home to Tyneside after all those years away. It was a great tale and one that everybody wanted the exclusive on.

I phoned Bob Harris, the journalist closest to Bobby and the man who'd ghosted his autobiography. Bob was a great guy and an esteemed journalist, who was well within his rights to tell me where to go when I politely asked if he wouldn't mind passing on Bobby's number or, at least, get a message to him. To Bob's eternal credit, he gave me the number, but with the caveat that Bobby wasn't talking to anybody at the time.

Oh well, nothing ventured, nothing gained, so I rang Bobby on his mobile and left a message on his voicemail. Within an hour, I got a call back, with Bobby saying he would be delighted to chat to me, and could I be at his house in Ipswich at 10 a.m. the next morning? When I reported back to Andy Melvin and my other Sky colleagues that I'd got Bobby, they were astonished, and it was easily the biggest scoop of my career up to then.

A cameraman and I arrived at Bobby's house the next day and we also had a courier bike on standby outside, waiting for the tape – as it was in those days – to rush it back to London to feed up the line. It was a Sunday and the morning's papers were all full of speculation, but nobody could stand the story up because Bobby hadn't said a word and nobody from Newcastle was commenting.

There were question marks, though, as to whether Bobby was over the hill and past his sell-by date, given he was sixty-six years old at the time. We set the cameras up, started the interview and, in his very first answer, he made an error which looked confusing and sounded awkward. Although he recovered and continued his sentence, it was really uncomfortable. It was an error which, had it been seen, could have supported those who were suspicious of him not being sharp enough for the job.

I turned to the cameraman and said, 'Let's hold it a minute, can you rewind and start again?' He said, 'If I do that, then we're going to lose all of that first answer.' I said, 'Exactly.' Because, in the back of my mind, had that even gone on the cutting-room floor, I *know* it would have ended up somewhere damaging. I've seen too many things over the years, which were never meant to see the light of day, mysteriously make it into newspapers; somebody has probably earned some money out of it. I wasn't willing to take that risk with Bobby because he was a man I admired and respected so much, and I wanted to make sure that footage did not exist in any form.

I have a fascination and an admiration for anybody who takes on the England job because, ultimately, it only ends one way, and the damage that it can do along the way can be so painful. Even those who emerge relatively unscathed will still look back and wonder if it was all worth it.

To be fair, Terry Venables left the England job with his reputation intact, and it was only after his bruising encounter with Alan Sugar at Spurs that he suffered something of a setback. It was during that time I got to know him well, and Di and I would sometimes go down to Terry's nightclub, Scribes, off Kensington High Street, where he would hold court on a Saturday night and where the great, the good and not so good of both the football and celebrity world would often gravitate.

Saturday night was karaoke night and, on this particular evening, Di and I found ourselves sitting on the same table as a whole host of different characters including the then-Wimbledon defender John Scales, as well as Swedish film star Britt Ekland, who had previously been married to Peter Sellers and who'd been Rod Stewart's partner for a couple of years.

To add to what was the usual eclectic mix of people, the former gangster and underworld hitman 'Mad' Frankie Fraser was also in attendance. The flamboyant agent Eric

'Monster' Hall was always master of ceremonies on these occasions, and I'd heard Terry take Eric to one side and make him promise this would be a low-key night and that no special attention would be paid to the fact that a man infamous for being a torturer was part of the Scribes clientele.

'No, absolutely Tel, no chance, stand on me, no monster, monster fuss.' Then, barely pausing for breath, Eric said, 'Right, tonight, ladies and gentlemen, it's karaoke night and to kick off proceedings, we've got "Mad" Frankie Fraser singing, "If I Had a Hammer".'

Terry's head was in his hands.

There are some managers who you simply cannot predict how they are going to behave or why they act that way. I'd regularly interviewed Louis van Gaal over the years from his time in the Champions League, and also because he'd taken part in the José Mourinho special documentary that Sky had put together. So when he arrived at Manchester United, I thought life would be pretty straightforward in terms of building a relationship. I could not have been more wrong.

I think the problem was, he took things so literally. I remember him walking towards me in the Old Trafford tunnel. We shook hands and, before the interview started, I said, 'How are you?' His response? 'I am fine and if I was not, I wouldn't tell you.'

As far as I know, I'd done nothing to piss him off or even irk him, it was just the way he was. In a pre-match, I was interviewing a manager and van Gaal was waiting off to one side, ready to step in as soon as the opposition boss had finished. Interview over, I said to the manager,

'Best of luck for today,' and he was off, back to his dressing room.

I then interviewed van Gaal and, after we finished, shook his hand and said, 'Good luck today.' 'What do you mean?' he said.

'You know, good luck, all the best for today.'

'No, you cannot be wishing me good luck.'

'Why not?'

'You wished the other manager good luck, you cannot be wishing me good luck, too.'

'Louis, it's just an expression.'

'Well, if you don't mean it, don't say it.' And he was gone, leaving me bemused and befuddled.

When I was making a documentary series called, *Godfathers of Football*, he was one of the subjects alongside Roy Hodgson, Claudio Ranieri, Sven-Göran Eriksson and Gerard Houllier. I travelled out to interview van Gaal in his home in Portugal, expecting the worst and certainly not an easy ride. Instead, he could not have been more welcoming, insisting I stay for a few glasses of wine after the interview. We've stayed in touch ever since, swapping messages on a regular basis.

ENGLAND'S FINEST. Two of the Premier League's greatest players,
Frank Lampard (*above*) and Steven Gerrard (*below*).
Both absolutely first class in my dealings with them, on and off camera.

GLOBAL ICONS. David Beckham (*above*) and Pelé (*below*) both gave us a fantastic night when they were recipients of the Legends of Football award.

SPECIAL ONES. José Mourinho (*above*) and Cristiano Ronaldo (*below*).
Portuguese men of more when it comes to silverware.
Both great to work with.

UP FOR DEBATE. Anchoring *The Debate* was always enjoyable. With Dennis Wise and Ian Wright (*above*), and a North London derby special with Arsenal fan, Piers Morgan, and former Spurs supremo, Alan Sugar.

GIVE US A BREAK MAN. Given how much he loves The Toon, it would have hurt Alan Shearer so much not being able to save them from relegation.

SHARPSHOOTER. Live with Paul Scholes, trying to capture the instant reaction and drama on the pitch. One of the best parts of the job.

EYES ON THE PRIZE. For me, the Premier League is still the hardest trophy to win anywhere in the world (*left*).

ENTENTE CORDIALE . . . MAINLY! I've probably interviewed Arsène Wenger more than any other Premier League manager over the last three decades (*above*).

RVP MVP. Robin Van Persie and Legends of Football 2016 co-host Rachel Riley after the Dutchman's goal was voted greatest Premier League goal of all time by his contemporaries (*below*).

JACK ON THE BOX. Interviewing Jack Grealish on the pitch after the Manchester City star won his first Premier League title in 2022.

MY TEAM. Lottie, Di, Ellie and Jack.

9

The Unspoken Pact

Dennis Wise was serious – deadly serious. 'Let me down over this, Geoff, and that's you and me finished. I mean it.' Where Wisey is concerned, that's a warning that always registers.

It was 1999, and we were sitting in one of the dressing rooms of Chelsea's former training ground out by Heathrow Airport. We had actually just finished an interview that had three potential outcomes. It could be a fantastic scoop, a brilliant exclusive; it might never see the light of day; or potentially it might have serious ramifications in a relationship with one of my best contacts.

I'd been tipped by a solid FA source that Wisey was getting a recall into the England squad after three years out in the cold. It was a remarkable story. Glenn Hoddle hadn't fancied him, a fall-out from their time together at Chelsea, but Kevin Keegan knew he needed his combative presence and wanted him back in the fold.

Armed with this information, I took a gamble. It was a Friday and Chelsea were away at Middlesbrough the next day. I knew the team would be flying north mid-afternoon and there would be no chance of getting hold of Wisey for an interview once the news of his call-up broke that afternoon.

I headed over to the training ground, where I grabbed Dennis as he came off the pitch. I explained what I needed, a word with the man who would be the biggest story from the squad, and that there was only a small window of opportunity to get it.

Frankly, Wisey did not believe for a moment his England career was about to be revived. He hadn't heard a word from Keegan or anybody at the FA to tip him the wink and he was less than certain an interview was necessarily the best thing to do but . . . To his eternal credit, he agreed to do a piece to camera, talking about his delight at the news and how he thought his international days were over.

Then came the warning that if he wasn't in the squad for some reason and there was even the hint he'd done an interview, a relationship built up over the best part of a decade would be destroyed in an instant.

Throughout my career, from my quasi-floor-manager days, through to taking the first steps as a reporter and to my current Sky role, I have always adhered to the old journalistic adage that the stories that make your career are the ones that you never use. In short, you see or hear things that players and managers do or say in your company, confident that you wouldn't use them. They are comfortable in your company, knowing you are only on duty when you both agree. Dennis had been good to me and we'd done some great shoots together, like the pre-FA Cup final piece where we'd driven him around London in an open-top Rolls-Royce Silver Ghost, then ending up in a rowboat on the Serpentine. Wisey got what Sky was about and I was determined not to jeopardize the bond we had.

So I promised him with everything that was dear to me that, in the event my FA tip was wrong, all footage of the interview would be binned and neither of us would breathe a word about it. With that, he joined the rest of the Chelsea lads for the trip to Middlesbrough and I hot-footed it back to Sky HQ with the tape. Now it was down to waiting for the squad announcement on the news wires.

Late afternoon, we're all in the Sky Sports newsroom when the squad dropped and, thank God, Dennis was included. Everyone was amazed at his inclusion and of course the first shout was that we had to find some way to get hold of him, only to be followed by a mood of despondency when it became obvious Chelsea were already ensconced in their Teesside hotel and inaccessible.

Casually, I said to our producer, Alan Mitchell, 'Mitch, I've got to get on the road but here's a tape, have a look and see what you think.' I was literally only seconds down the A4 when the phone rang, and it was Mitch. 'That's brilliant, but how the fuck did you get it?'

To be honest, I got lucky with a couple of things, but I would add I had worked hard to make that luck. First, it could all have gone out the window if my FA source had made a mistake, but he was a contact I had spent a lot of time with so that's why he was willing to give me the nod.

Second, because of the rapport I'd built up with Dennis over the years, I could get him to take a punt. He judged me as someone that wouldn't let him down. Ask any reporter, broadcast or print, and they will tell you that you live or die by your contacts and the fundamental question of trust. It goes to the very heart of my relationship with players.

The top stars simply don't *have* to engage wholeheartedly if they don't want to. Yes, there's the post-match instant response, but I'm talking more about the kind of interviews where they are happy to open up and give 'of themselves'. Television interviews, by their very nature, depend on that willingness from the subject to buy into the interview, because there's no ability to write round it as there would be for a print journalist.

Newspaper and television interviews have the same aim editorially but are very different beasts. Take post-match, for instance. The television reporter is stood at arm's length away from a manager in an intimate one-to-one situation, trying to get the first response on the most important issues of the day in a limited amount of time. As the first reaction you quite often have to take the hit of a manager's wrath, with him furious at being asked a certain question, but the simple fact is he will be asked it anyway in the other press conference situations.

That manager will then go to the newspaper press conference where you might have half a dozen reporters firing questions; it's not simply down to one person to get the best and most appropriate angle.

From the moment he broke into the first team at Liverpool, I got on brilliantly with Steven Gerrard. I benefited from the fact that Gary McAllister, who I'd got to know through Alan Smith as they were both together at Leicester, put in a good word for me with Stevie. Gary said I could be trusted, which is an excellent referral, but only Stevie would ultimately decide if that were true.

Stevie was unfailingly excellent with me and was always willing, amongst undoubtedly dozens of requests, to make time for Sky.

When he was approached to make a DVD about a year in his life, I was pleased to be chosen to do the section where you spend a day with him away from the pitch. Driving past his old school, seeing the house where he was brought up, that sort of thing. However, neither of us look back with any pride at the game of pool we played for the cameras at Liverpool's old Melwood training ground, given we were both utterly useless and the game lasted longer than a frame of snooker.

We had a solid working relationship. He also knew that when he was sent off after just 38 seconds in his final match against Manchester United, that I wouldn't necessarily hound him to death over the red card, but that I would push him, and he accepted that. In fact, in later years we've discussed situations, and he said he would be almost offended if my questions didn't have an edge. It's the same now he is a manager.

I never, though, mistake this kind of working relationship for friendship. That certainly doesn't mean you aren't friendly, far from it, but you aren't ringing each other every week just to see how they're doing, like you do with your mates. There is an unwritten contract that, at times, a player needs you as much as you need him. It's a business deal, in essence, but with a deep-seated mutual respect. The beauty is that if one of us steps over the line – and this goes for many players and managers – it doesn't mean the relationship is destroyed for ever; it might just need a little time to heal the wounds.

My overriding memory of interviewing Gerrard was pitch-side in Istanbul, just moments after Liverpool had won the Champions League in 2005. It's not the best interview I've ever done, but just the sense of wonder in his eyes makes it for me, the way he looks around the stadium at the euphoria of the Liverpool fans and what it means to them. He tells me he still gets goosebumps whenever he sees that replayed, not because of the brilliance of either my questions or his answers, simply the fact it's a moment in his life that will define his time at Anfield.

It's a similar situation with Frank Lampard. I never bought into the theory that he and Stevie couldn't play in the same midfield for England; I think a good manager would have seen how they complemented each other rather than focusing on their similarities. Where they are similar, though, is in their outlook to the game and life.

Frank never shied away from an interview, he never ducked a tough situation or shirked his responsibilities as a senior member of the Chelsea and England squads. And when he made the transformation from player to manager, he didn't expect any special treatment from me, even though we'd built up a strong relationship over the years. When things were tough for him at Chelsea, he made it clear that he expected me not to go easy on him, saying, 'Ask the questions you need to.'

It's not all tough questions and soul-searching answers,

though; sometimes it can be a lot of fun. Frank had been approached by *The Sun* to do a TV advert for their Super Goals pull-out, which was going to be shown in the build-up to one season, with the shoot comprising him answering questions from a reporter about the paper's football coverage.

His agent, Steve Kutner, approached me and said that Frank would like me to be the reporter because he'd feel more comfortable with me around rather than an actor or one of *The Sun*'s guys. Unfortunately, the shoot coincided with my holiday in the south of France so, when the paper rang me, I had to apologize for my absence.

I thought nothing more of it and was relaxing in France when Steve rang me. 'Geoff, Frank really wants you there if you can make it,' he said. 'Sorry, Steve, I'm on holiday, no can do. It's more than my life's worth.'

'I get that,' he replied, 'but you'd be doing Frank a favour.'

'I know, and I'm sorry pal, you know how it is.'

'They're paying X.'

All of a sudden, I was available! And that was it: holiday in France paid for – and the next one.

There have been more than a few surreal moments, especially when you're dealing with football royalty – and that's exactly what Andriy Shevchenko was in his homeland of Ukraine. I wouldn't say we were close when he was at Chelsea, but I'd interviewed him a number of times and we struck up a rapport. I was struck by just how he carried himself. Here was a man who became a legend at AC Milan and whom Roman Abramovich had personally approached to bring him to the Premier League, yet he possessed such humility and understated class.

Things didn't really work out for him at Stamford Bridge but, when he returned to Milan on loan, we stayed in semi-regular touch – so much so that when he signed permanently for Dinamo Kyiv, he was happy for me to go out to Ukraine and do quite a big feature on him.

The idea was to retrace his steps, from a child starting out in the game to this triumphant homecoming, the hero's return. It couldn't have gone much better as Shevchenko took us back to his first club, an obscure ground several miles from his old house, and he took us along the forest paths he trod as a ten year old just to go training – lovely stuff.

The final part of the shoot took us to the Dinamo stadium, and we were travelling in two cars, Shevchenko and me in his Porsche, with my cameraman Ben Bregman and Sheva's bodyguard – who made Tyson Fury look like Ronnie Corbett – following behind in a Mercedes SUV. All was going well until a woman a few hundred yards up the road suddenly decided to pull a U-turn in the middle of a dual carriageway. It was impossible to avoid a collision and Andriy and I ploughed into her.

Miraculously, nobody was hurt but, as we all waited at the side of the road for the emergency services and recovery vehicles, a slew of TV crews and photographers arrived at the scene and started snapping away until the bodyguard, with a nod from Sheva, asked them politely to leave. None of them were about to argue.

A little while later, a replacement car was sent, and we carried on our journey. No sooner had we got in the car then Andriy's phone started ringing every few seconds. Obviously, the news had broken about the smash and was being played on a loop on Ukraine's rolling news channel. It even reached England and I received a call from the Sky desk, not asking if I was OK, but if I could get a few words with Shevchenko about the accident!

At one stage, he took four calls in quick succession, all of which seemed to be people he knew well, and all of which he answered in Italian. Of course, I didn't understand a word, so when there was a lull in the incessant buzzing of his phone, I said, 'Go on then, who was that on the line?'

He smiled, 'Nobody really, just some friends.'

'Come on, who was it?' I persisted.

'Well, the first call was Franco Baresi. The second was Silvio Berlusconi. The third one was Paolo Maldini. And the last one was Giorgio Armani. The news has broken in Italy and they were worried about me.'

Global superstars do take a degree of different handling. Again, it comes down to the fact that they simply do not have to do any media unless it interests them, and there's nobody at their clubs who is going to tell them otherwise. The knack, then, is to pique their interest with something new and something different.

I'd been given some time with Cristiano Ronaldo before Manchester United's Champions League final against Barcelona in 2009. I'd interviewed Ronaldo numerous times before, and while he was perfectly co-operative, he was essentially guarded and studious in choosing his words.

At the time, there were huge question marks over his United future, with Real Madrid lurking in the background. The match was billed as a showdown between Ronaldo and Messi, and the United media team were having kittens over the interview's content, insisting firmly that the only topic up for discussion was the final, absolutely nothing else.

I appreciated their position but there had to be some degree of journalistic integrity to the interview, otherwise they may as well have just paid for some advertising space on the channel. Tap-dancing delicately, I arrived for the interview with my best reporter's jacket, a clipboard and a pair of glasses plus a plan in mind.

We set up the cameras and lighting and when Ronaldo entered the room, I took him to one side and said, 'Today, you're going to answer every question about the final, your future and your battle with Lionel Messi next week because you're going to be interviewed by somebody you love and admire.'

'OK, who?' he replied, sounding intrigued.

'You,' I said, taking off my jacket and handing it to him, along with the clipboard and the glasses.

The idea was to try and get the best out of Ronaldo by Ronaldo interviewing himself. I gave him a list of questions which he rattled off down the camera before switching positions and then him answering the questions as if from himself. Some slick editing gave us the perfect package, with Ronaldo talking about Messi, the final, his penalty technique, before insisting he would be at Old Trafford the following season.

He joined Madrid two months later.

While understanding the relationship between journalist and player is a business one for the vast majority of the time, there are occasions when it crosses into friendship, and that's how I would class Alan Shearer now, as a mate.

It dates back to the early days, even before the Premier League started in 1992. It didn't take the brains of a rocket scientist to see this kid at Southampton was special and was obviously going to have a massive impact on the game. There was just something about him, an absolute dedication to the art of scoring goals that singled him out.

I arranged to get him on Sky a couple of times and then, when he joined Blackburn, and Sky were covering them a lot more, we developed a strong rapport. There were people at the channel who doubted the wisdom of having him as a studio guest because all they saw was the public persona, which was being carefully managed by Shearer's then agent, Tony Stephens.

I say managed, but really it was being mismanaged. Stephens had a superb stable of players, including Shearer and David Platt, both of whom were great fun, excellent company and could tell stories all day, but the public never saw any of that because of the way they were handled. Any newspaper columns were stripped bare of charisma by Stephens and his fellow agents, who wouldn't let a syllable into the paper if it even hinted at basic human emotion or anything approaching an opinion. 'Great player but dull' was the common consensus.

It was the same with us at Sky. Shearer was the England captain, and the FA were launching a new kit and had got us along to film and promote the launch. Now the ideal shot is Shearer looking at the shirt and then pulling it over his head to reveal the Three Lions, the design and the Umbro badge, as it was back then. Nothing too controversial with that, you'd think, all very straightforward and cosy:

Sky get an exclusive and the FA get their publicity for the new kit. Job's a good 'un.

Except that Shearer's management sent a note insisting that we only film once Shearer had the shirt on. The reason? Just in case we filmed some underarm hair. I kid you not.

That kind of attitude did Alan a huge disservice because he was as sharp as a tack and smart enough to avoid the kind of curly questions from reporters that might get him into trouble. The whole 'boring' tag followed him for too long, but there was no telling Stephens and company. They seemed quite content to let the finest striker in the world carry that kind of baggage.

At Sky, we all began to work on his television technique, showing him the best way of analysing match action, getting him to explain everything from a player's perspective with the insight only a pro can bring. We worked on his delivery style, the way he spoke down the camera, and how to do a live cross from pitchside back to the studio.

And he got it immediately because he was savvy and knew what was required from him. He was also incredibly accommodating to me after he joined Newcastle and always went the extra mile for Sky.

In those days, the interviews were still all recorded on tape; no digital feed down a line to London, you had to physically have the tape in your hand in order to package it. All well and good if you're filming in London or Manchester where we had easy access to editing suites, but there were no facilities like that in Newcastle if I needed to interview Al.

Thanks to him, that was never a problem. I'd get the

first flight out of Heathrow to Newcastle, no bags required and, while I was in the air, Alan would already be at the hotel across the road from Newcastle Airport, where he'd be sat with a cameraman, mic'd up and waiting. He is always fifteen minutes early for anything and hates lateness. I'd get off the plane, walk out of the airport and across the road to the hotel, do the interview, pick up the tape and be back in the airport to catch the same plane back down to London. The cabin staff would look at me and ask, 'Didn't you just get off this plane?' but it was as easy as booking an Uber is these days.

The fella hasn't changed a bit in all the time I've known him. Whenever a withheld number comes on my phone, it's only ever one of three people. If it's Shearer, he'll always start the conversation the same way, with a bellowed, 'NOW THEN'. And then he's off, ripping the piss out of me or offering the latest gossip, no different to during his playing days.

You can't relax around him; always have to be on your toes. He hates sitting around and always has to be doing something productive – and expects those around him to be the same. I remember staying at his house in Newcastle after we'd been to a dinner the night before, a night that, predictably, had gone on into the early hours. I was expecting a bit of a lie-in to recover when, on the dot of seven, he burst into my room with a cup of tea in his hand and the immortal words, 'Come on, fat boy, it's time you were up.' Pleading for a bit more kip did no good. 'You can sleep when you're dead,' was his astute observation. To him, life is to be lived because you're a long time looking at the lid.

Towards the end of his career, but while there were still a good few miles left in his legs, we were sitting in a car and I idly asked whether he fancied a taste of life abroad. The Keegan era was over, there didn't seem much chance he'd win any more silverware, and a couple of seasons in Spain ought to have been appealing because there would definitely have been some takers.

He just turned to me and said, 'It's just not possible for you to understand how much it means to me to be Newcastle's number nine. You'll never truly know what this club means to me and how happy I am to be amongst my own people, with all my family around me. It's everything I've ever wanted, and I couldn't be happier anywhere else.'

That, to me, is the mark of the man. The wonderful and sadly missed Ray Harford once said that Shearer is the type of person you'd be proud to welcome if your daughter brought him home. When I first started doing regular stuff with Shearer, Kevin Keegan pulled me and said, 'You've got Alan's trust, he doesn't give that lightly and he doesn't do second chances.' I thought it was an odd thing to say at the time but it's perfectly accurate. He is naturally sceptical of people but also one of the most generous and supportive people you could wish to meet. His goal-scoring records and honours are special but, personally, I think he should be equally proud of The Alan Shearer Foundation, which he started in 2006. He has raised millions of pounds and improved beyond belief so many lives of seriously disadvantaged people.

One time, I was giving a talk at a local school on the subject of ambition and career paths. I needed some examples or words that would inspire, so I phoned Alan.

He gave me the perfect motivational quote which I relayed to the students. 'Listen, I've trained and played with players who, technically, have far more ability than me. They had all the tricks in the world and all the natural ability, but what they don't have is a mindset like mine. I'm a stubborn Geordie bastard. In my opinion, to succeed in life, it takes more will than skill.'

Strangely, one of the other players I grew closest to during his career was a man who had more fall-outs with Shearer than possibly any other. Craig Bellamy is probably one of the most interesting characters I've ever met in the game and the fact he is, at times, the polar opposite to Shearer, makes him all the more fascinating to me.

The pair simply didn't get on during their Newcastle days. Judging from his autobiography, Craig resented the plaudits Alan was still receiving towards the end of his career when he believed he was carrying the workload in their partnership. I don't think Alan was overly impressed with Craig's attitude at times, either.

To be honest, Craig rubbed me up the wrong way when I first encountered him. In fact, everybody I know was irritated by Bellers when they first met him; he's just that kind of character. In terms of a slow build as a contact, this one didn't even set off at a snail's pace. He didn't like the media and, as far as he was concerned, I was Shearer's mate. Double whammy.

He was available for interview if you asked him but, when he turned up, he was stand-offish, brusque, always on the verge of a short word if you strayed into territory where he didn't want to go. It's a phrase I've used before in this chapter, but he simply didn't give 'of himself' in any way which, given how intelligent and insightful he can be, was a shame.

It didn't help our relationship when post Arsenal versus Newcastle, a studio discussion about his absence from the line-up turned towards his attitude. I hadn't been involved, but I was the one he phoned to vent his spleen, raging against the injustice of it all and making it clear he was less than impressed with Sky. It was a tough few minutes.

But as I got to know him well and he began to be more trusting before, during and after our interviews, I began to get an insight into what was driving him. His intensity was fuelled by two factors: his obsession with being the very best footballer he could be, and not wasting an ounce of the talent he'd been given. It was an obsession with him, and rarely have I seen anybody harder on himself or on teammates if he feels for a second standards are slipping. Mentally, he beats himself up if he falls even a step below the levels he has set.

Much of that obsession is a product of the depression he has suffered since childhood. It was a privilege to sit alongside him on a programme I hosted for Sky during Covid called *Off Script*. One episode dealt with mental health and the ways it impacts a player's life. Craig was searingly honest, not for a moment hesitating when revealing the depths to which he sank during his career. It was astonishing to hear how he'd had to come up with coping methods over the years, including requesting to train alone in the afternoons because being around other people was so traumatic that he was unable to even face his teammates and pretend life was normal. How he maintained a top-class career when the effects of his illness were so debilitating is difficult to comprehend.

The fact he did have an excellent career is testimony to him and his work ethic. These days, he applies that same passion and commitment to coaching but is a far more rounded and contented person, even if he does hammer me for being a constant name-dropper!

Having got to know and respect Bellers, I felt obligated to step in after the horrific news of Gary Speed's death in 2011 reached me. Alan Shearer called a few hours before the news became public and I've never heard him so upset; through his grief, he let me know that Gary – who I'd also got to know quite well and had been a Sky guest many times – had passed.

Immediately I thought of Craig because he hero-worshipped Gary and held him up as the epitome of the player and person Bellers himself wanted to be. Liverpool were playing Manchester City that day and I knew what an impact the news would have on Craig and that a match would be the absolute last thing on his mind.

I got hold of Steve Clarke, who was Kenny Dalglish's number two at Liverpool, apologized for disturbing him on a match day, but asked if he could get Kenny to ring me urgently. A few minutes later, Kenny was on the line. He hadn't heard the news about Gary but when I explained how I thought it would impact Craig mentally, he took control immediately. He made sure Bellers was protected, taking him out of the squad that day and then doing everything in his power to help him through one of the toughest times in Craig's life.

I always felt it should have been Sir Kenny Dalglish

before he was knighted, not just for his legendary football achievements but for the incredible manner in which he led Liverpool in the aftermath of the Hillsborough disaster. The compassion, leadership, and dignity he displayed were absolutely outstanding.

Reading this back, it feels like everything associated with Craig is either angst or anguish and that's certainly not the case. He is the king of the wind-up, with the perfect poker face that puts even those who know him well off balance.

I was supposed to be interviewing him in Cardiff when he moved back to Wales but was then diverted onto another job. My colleague, Pat Davidson, was sent in my place. I phoned Craig the night before to let him know about the switch and, after enduring the predictable, 'Oh, you're too big time to come down to Cardiff, are you?', suggested there might be a little fun to be had.

When Pat turned up the next day, he was met with, 'Who are you? Where's Shreevesie?' From experience, the last thing you need minutes before an interview is a player in a foul mood, so the usual method is to placate them the best way possible. So Pat was in overdrive, telling Craig how much he was looking forward to the interview and how much he admired Craig as a player.

Bellers, though, was having none of it. 'You don't get it, do you?' he said. 'When I do interviews, I do them with Geoff Shreeves and nobody else. I don't even know who you are. What did you say your name was?'

Now, I've been there with Craig when he's in full flow and it's an uncomfortable experience, especially if you don't know him, because he can be utterly convincing. Fortunately, he couldn't keep it up, and burst out laughing moments later, explaining the situation to an utterly relieved Pat who then went on to get an excellent interview. He phoned me on the way back up the M4 and his first words were, 'You fucker!'

Vinnie Jones and I grew up in the same neck of the woods in Hertfordshire and even played against each other in the County Cup youth final when St Albans City beat his Watford Youth 2-1. We would have been around sixteen at the time and Vinnie was already six foot-plus, with a full beard and earrings, so you could say he stood out.

He, of course, progressed from local football through to Wimbledon and their FA Cup final success and into the birth of the Premier League. He was in the great 'Alive and Kicking' advert for Sky, with twenty-one other players from the different clubs launching that first season but, apparently, forgot his boots, had to wear a pair two sizes too small, and then lost his boot deal because they were the wrong brand!

Vinnie was always up for doing interviews and shoots with us. He embraced the life of the Premier League to its fullest and there was no edge to him; if he wanted to do something, he threw himself into it with amazing gusto. He knew he wasn't the best player in the world, he recognized his shortcomings, but I've never met anybody who worked harder, day-in and day-out, to make the most of his opportunity.

He loved his reputation as a tough guy, but he was never happier than when he was out in the fields. Vinnie would lose himself in the countryside, tending to game birds, walking through the woods with his dogs and basically living the life of a gamekeeper. It was about as far removed from professional football as it could be, and it would be fascinating to join him and listen to his stories of the countryside and wildlife.

So we agreed to meet at his dad Pete's smallholding in Colney Heath. We'd finished an interview previewing Wimbledon's game against Arsenal at Highbury (where Vinnie would score as sweet a half-volley as you could wish to see) and I asked if he would do me a favour. It was the early years of me helping to raise money for the Nordoff Robbins charity for musical therapy – more of which later – and I wanted Vinnie to do a little promotional video to play on the night of the event to encourage people to bid in the auction.

It was a bit of a skit on his hard-man image, where he looked straight down the barrel of the camera and said, in his most menacing voice, 'Right, listen you lot, we're supposed to be raising money for Nordoff Robbins tonight, so get your hands in your pocket otherwise I'll be up there to have a word with ya.' Well, he delivered this monologue to camera in one take and he was absolutely fantastic.

I said, 'Not being funny, Vin, but you were really good at that. Have you ever thought about doing stuff?' 'Funny you should say that,' he replied, 'but I've got a mate who asked me to be in a film called *Lock, Stock and Two Smoking Barrels*. I did it for a bit of fun, you never know where it's going to lead.' To date, Vinnie has appeared in 110 movies.

One of the premieres for his 2020 film, *The Big Ugly*, was held at a cinema in Berkhamsted, purely for all Vinnie's friends and family from Hertfordshire, and I was pleased to be invited. Resplendent in Hollywood-style black tie,

Vinnie seemed to be in his element, smiling and shaking hands, loving the fact all his mates from the old days could be a part of his night.

But there was something about him that worried me. I watched him pretty closely during the evening and he was off, not the same Vinnie I'd got to know over the years. He was smiling but the smile never reached his eyes. This was about a year after his wonderful wife, Tanya, had passed away from cancer and I suspected this was having more of an impact than Vinnie was letting on publicly. There had been a scene in the movie where his character's partner dies, and I wondered if it had triggered something in him that had lain dormant for a while but had now risen to the surface. Guesswork on my part, I could be completely wrong.

When I got home that night, I messaged him. I apologized if he felt I was out of line, but I said I was worried about him and that there appeared to be something missing in him that night. He immediately messaged back, 'How did you know?'

The fact is, I recognized in Vinnie what I'd felt myself when I was suffering from depression after my illness. There was a sense of dislocation, of feeling like you're functioning normally but always being one step removed from normality, and doing your best to kid yourself you're fine while being pretty far from fine.

We messaged back and forth that night and over the next day and, little by little, he admitted he was struggling badly; he wasn't coping. The fact is, nobody can tell you how or when to grieve and loss is such a destructive force. One of the things he wrote really hit home. He said, 'I'm in a fight at the moment but I can't see the fucker in front of me.'

A few months later, someone rang me and said that they'd just heard Vinnie talking on Five Live about his mental health battles and the fact he'd been seeing a therapist as a result of our conversation. It was the very least I could do.

There are times when you get to know a player so well that you might just inadvertently cross the line. From the moment he broke into the Chelsea team, John Terry was great to work with. We did so many interviews and shoots together over the years. When he moved into his new house in Surrey, he built a trout lake and he couldn't have been happier conducting an interview with rod in hand.

Chelsea won their first Premier League title under José Mourinho away at Bolton and the next week I was at Stamford Bridge filming a live link into *Soccer AM*. Out of the corner of my eye, I spy John Terry and Joe Cole, armed with water bottles, and they start squirting me while I'm live on air. Having had their laugh, they scarper away down the tunnel, cackling like schoolkids.

Anyway, I wrap up the link and we're putting the camera and sound equipment away when my phone rang. It was my pal David Piper who works in football sponsorship and marketing and had been at Bournemouth as a kid. 'What the fuck were you thinking of?' was the startled enquiry. 'What? What do you mean?' I replied. 'Trying to break our captain's leg a couple of hours before kick-off. Have a look back at it.'

So, I got VT to play the footage back and I just froze. As JT and Joe ran past me, without any hesitation I'd stuck out my leg in an attempt to trip John. Luckily, he skipped over my leg, otherwise he would have gone sprawling down a flight of concrete steps and I'd have been guilty of injuring the Chelsea and England captain and all the ramifications that would have brought.

You can take the boy out of Sunday football, I guess.

I've forgotten many nights with Niall Quinn but that's because I've made the mistake of going out drinking with him. He is one of the most engaging people I've ever met, with a livewire brain that fizzes with ideas. It's little surprise to me that he's made such a fabulously successful life for himself away from the game.

He was always an articulate and considered guest on Sky and we used him a lot over the years because of the intelligence he brought to any conversation. He's also a compelling storyteller and one of the most persuasive and well-connected men on the planet. He had me doubled up when, over a midday pint of Guinness, he said that he'd been out with a senior figure in the Catholic Church of England the night before and had ended up selling him half a greyhound!

He is also beyond generous. He was the first player to give away the income raised from his testimonial, which came as no surprise to people who know him. There was also a time at Sky when I was unsure of my future and where I stood. Niall sensed there was something amiss and I explained the position I was in. His response will always stay with me. 'Geoff, you know I run a few businesses. If anything goes wrong, I'll find you a place somewhere on the same salary as Sky are paying you for two years to make sure you get back on your feet.'

You simply do not forget things like that. Sheer class.

I'm happy to say that I've formed and enjoy similar relationships with many of the current top Premier League players and managers. I'd like to think that, over the years, we'll develop the same sense of trust I have with their predecessors mentioned here. I don't kid myself; I'm not going to pretend I can talk about some of the things with the new generation as I did with players closer to my age, but the very fact I'm in a tunnel or at the side of the pitch every weekend and midweek at least makes me a familiar face. Football is at the very heart of player–reporter relationships and will always be so.

10

Legends of Football

Football can be a brutal business. Decent people get cast aside and forgotten; reputations that have taken years to build are too often shredded overnight while the relentless demand for success – in whatever form that takes – puts intolerable pressure on individuals, to the point where they make foolish and ill-conceived decisions that have unhealthy ramifications.

But there is another side to the football industry; it can be utterly transformative. When you've seen David Beckham, Gareth Southgate or Arsène Wenger interacting with people whose lives too often verge on the intolerable, and they help create moments of joy, you realize that football, for all its myriad faults, can be an incredible force for good.

For over two decades, I've helped stage an annual gala dinner where we honour an outstanding recipient from the football world in order to raise money for Nordoff Robbins, a charity that provides music therapy. The charity is strongly supported by the music industry to help those on whom life has taken its toll. It can be those who are suffering from brain damage, dementia, or in particular autism; people who find the everyday too overwhelming, violent, or simply just too manic and loud to cope with.

It's astonishing to see just how music helps those individuals communicate, relax, and find just a semblance of balance in a world that can be for them tumultuous at best. That the football world has also embraced the charity probably means as much as anything I might have achieved in my career. To be able to call somebody up and tell them we want to celebrate their life in the game, and all that we ask in return is a little time devoted to the charity, and then to be met by open arms, speaks volumes for an industry that has a reputation for sometimes lacking soul.

I was fortunate to be involved from the very early days. Musical PR guru Gary Farrow recommended Richard Keys be asked to host the event, who in turn told the organizers that it might be a good move to bring me in as more of a link between players and managers, an extension of my day job with Sky, if you like.

At the time HMV were the country's largest music retailer and having something of a crisis of conscience where Nordoff Robbins was concerned. It was the industry's main charity, but it didn't receive the kind of support it truly merited from the high street record-selling giant. It was a bit ad hoc, nothing structured.

Thankfully, the chief executive of HMV, Brian McLaughlin, decided there had to be a concerted effort to raise both funding and awareness for something that did so much good. Brian, along with fellow HMV colleagues Jim Peal and Glenn Ward, attended a traditional dinner with speakers at Enfield Town Football Club. It was from there that they realized the obvious vehicle to use was football, and it certainly helped that we were four years into the Premier League. The game had become synonymous with glamour, with a reach and reputation that was growing by the season.

For me, it was the perfect opportunity, bringing together the two biggest passions in my life. The crossover between football and the music industry has been a rich seam that Sky has mined for three decades and one that I've been delighted to be involved with. Like so many teenagers, all I lived for was football and music at school and (however briefly!) college. One day I wanted to be Gerry Francis, the next Paul Weller against the backdrop of some fantastic teenage years.

I'm not sure it's the other way round, but so many rock stars and musicians are frustrated footballers. Rod Stewart was on the books of Brentford as a youngster but, as he told me when I interviewed him ahead of an Old Firm game, it was either get up early and train with Brentford or lie in and work at night. Fair to say, Rod is not a morning person.

Not that he's given up on football, far from it. He has an encyclopaedic knowledge of his beloved Celtic, and his former residence, a palatial Essex house on the edge of Epping Forest, is home to a full-sized pitch that would not look out of place at a Premier League training ground. When we did the Old Firm shoot there, he was in full flow, loving life and talking about all the great games around the world he'd seen. That shoot also had the added advantage of us being served bacon sandwiches for breakfast by Rod's beautiful model wife, Rachel Hunter, at the end of it.

The connection between football and music has also provided some of the more unusual and surprising moments in my life, like the time when I was driving with my wife, Di, and the phone rang in the car. I didn't recognize the number but nearly swerved off the road when the voice at the other end of it said, 'Hello, Geoff, this is Elton.'

I'd read Elton John's autobiography and loved it so much that I'd asked the Watford chairman, Scott Duxbury, to pass on a note saying so. I think Elton must have asked Scott for my number and simply phoned up to chat football. His passion and knowledge is second to none and, wherever he is in the world, he organizes to have Watford games screened live, as well as matches from Spain, France, Italy and Germany. Football feels like the most harmless addiction he's ever had.

Actually, I wish I had Elton's influence when it comes to watching games anywhere in the world, it might have helped me grant a favour for another group of rock stars. In just the second year of Sky's Premier League coverage, I was at home one night when the phone rang. Di picked it up and then told me there was somebody who wanted to speak to me.

'Who is it?' I asked.

'Some bloke called something Elliott, I think he said,' Di replied.

So I picked up. 'Hello.'

'Hello, Geoff, this is Joe Elliott.'

'Sorry?'

'Joe Elliott, lead singer of Def Leppard. We're touring in Canada at the moment, and we can't find anywhere to watch Sheffield Wednesday versus Sheffield United in the FA Cup semi-final. I'm a Blade and Rick Savage is a Wednesdayite. Can Sky help out?'

Now, I have no idea where he got my number from and, despite my making genuine enquiries, unfortunately we couldn't help them out with a trans-Atlantic feed, no matter how devoted they were to their beloved teams.

So while the chance to get involved with Nordoff Robbins appealed to me, I was a little sceptical after some of the things I'd heard about people in the music industry and their – shall we say – lack of reliability. Thankfully, Brian put my mind at rest when we met up for lunch, although he reckons it was only after the fourth bottle of champagne that I was truly convinced!

The HMV trio of executives took the plunge, underwriting and organizing a sporting night, with Jimmy Greaves doing his one-man show. They'd hired the ballroom at the Grosvenor Hotel on Park Lane but had partitioned the room off just in case they couldn't fill it. But come the night, they'd sold 500 tickets, Greavsie was in brilliant form, and they ended up raising about £50,000 with ticket sales, an auction and a raffle. Suddenly, there was a real appetite to do something even bigger and better. Alan Zafer brought production expertise, Steve Knott – another HMV executive – joined the committee, and Jim's daughter Rae became our excellent event organizer.

The first event held under the banner of 'Football

Extravaganza' was in honour of John Charles in 1997. The Welsh legend was deeply moved to be asked to be the recipient, but initially was going to decline because he didn't own a dinner suit at the time. It was a ridiculously small price to pay to buy him a new suit in order for him to attend, and the night was a fantastic success.

Over the next two years, the success of the event grew and grew as we recognized Sir Stanley Matthews and Nat Lofthouse. Both nights saw a thousand people in the room, and we were becoming established as a highlight in football's social calendar, as well as raising huge sums for Nordoff Robbins. But there was definitely a feeling we had to bring things slightly more up to date with a more contemporary figure.

Brian Clough more than deserved the recognition. Back-to-back European Cup titles with Nottingham Forest, the league title with Derby County and a host of other cup victories would have secured his place in the pantheon even without his outspoken and often outrageous views, none of which he ever held back. Charismatic and entertaining, we felt he was the perfect recipient.

The added bonus was that he appeared to have his drinking under control in the seven years since he retired from football, after his Forest side were relegated in the first season of the Premier League. Away from the incessant pressure of the game, Brian had found some much-needed equilibrium.

We approached him through both his son, Nigel, who is possibly one of the most decent people you could ever meet, and Brian's great friend, the former ITV commentator, Brian Moore. Both were fully supportive; both thought it would be a fine way to honour the great man and there didn't appear to be a single cloud on the horizon.

Well, not until I got a panicked phone call from Brian Moore three days before the event. One of his best-known lines of commentary described Ronald Koeman's free kick, which ended England's World Cup hopes under Graham Taylor – 'He's going to flick it, he's going to flick it' – and our conversation was almost a carbon copy of that. 'Geoff, he's back on it, he's back on it.' Apparently, Cloughie had chosen that week, of all weeks, to hit the bottle again – and in a way that jeopardized his appearance at our event.

With an impending sense of doom, I contacted Nigel, and he outlined in no uncertain terms that he didn't feel it was right to put his dad in the spotlight and potentially expose him to ridicule. Riddled with guilt, I implored Nigel not to make a hasty decision, to give it a couple of days to see how Brian was coping. Of course, I understood the family's concerns and, if the roles were reversed, I would have felt exactly the same, so we found a compromise. All Brian had to do was attend, sit on the stage, and listen to people like Stuart Pearce paying tribute to him, as long as he was just on the stage and people could see him.

To Nigel's eternal credit, he agreed, and did his best to make sure Brian was at least in a fit state to attend. On the night, it was fair to say Brian hardly looked in the rudest of health, but he took his place on the stage with Keysie as master of ceremonies, and looked delighted with the sea of tributes that came his way over the course of the event.

Obviously fully aware that having Cloughie there but not speaking would have prompted some awkward questions, Keysie started to explain that Brian was feeling under the weather and wouldn't be speaking and asked if everybody could get to their feet and show their appreciation of a magnificent career.

Virtually before Keysie could finish his sentence, Cloughie was up, out of his seat, took the microphone and said, 'Give me that microphone, you bloody fool. Of course, I'm going to speak because I love London and it means, if I'm here, I'm usually picking up a trophy – or pissing all over Tottenham!' And he went on to do forty-five minutes in which he held the audience spellbound.

In the bar afterwards, I spotted Nigel. 'Told you it would be fine,' I laughed. His response, delivered with a smile, is probably best left completely off the record.

One of the things of which I'm most proud is the amount of money the evening has raised. Since 1997, we've been able to donate over £8.5 million to Nordoff Robbins and the work that has enabled them to do is beyond incredible. Much of the money raised comes via the auction we hold on the night, the magnificent prizes donated and the sublime brilliance of our auctioneers, the original being Nick Stewart.

Nick and I now enjoy a fantastic relationship. He's a former Guardsman and is known as The Colonel, although I call him Bagshot because he's so posh, and he refers to me as Baldrick in reference to what he claims are my oikish tendencies. Our first meeting, though, was far from auspicious.

Brian McLaughlin had invited a whole group of us to Cheltenham Races and Nick, in his MCC tie, was happily holding court on how he played golf at Sunningdale. He seemed to know everything and everyone concerned with cricket and horse racing. I fancied a horse in one of the later races called Top Cees, so I asked Nick what he thought of its chances. 'Not even in my vocabulary, old boy,' he insisted, airily dismissing it.

When the race started, I left the hospitality box to watch the race on the rails and, bugger me, if Top Cees didn't absolutely stroll it, without me having put a penny on. Back in the box, I started ranting at a few people, slaughtering Nick. 'Fucking bloke reckons he knows everything about everything: golf, horse racing, cricket. Says he's something to do with the music industry; well, I'd like to know what he's ever actually fucking done.'

Cue silence and a shuffling of feet before somebody quietly explained that Nick had discovered U2. Taxi for Shreeves.

Thanks to Nick's expertise, the auction has become one of the high points of what is now known, rightly, I believe, as 'Legends of Football'. At the Eric Cantona night in 2010, one of the prizes donated was a signed Cantona shirt, and the bidding was rolling along quite nicely. Five grand, eight, ten; the kind of money that an item normally gets on a night like this.

It starts to creep up a little bit more, and now I'm stood alongside Nick helping him to identify the football element in the room. We're at fourteen thousand and then fifteen with Fergie, sat on the top table, not particularly paying attention until Nick then said, 'We're at £17,000. Is that the final bid? Seventeen thousand from . . . Lady Cathy Ferguson.'

And suddenly, Alex is out of his seat. 'What are you

doing? I can get one of those every day of the week for nothing,' he yelped. But Cathy was insistent; she wanted that shirt so one or other of her grandkids could sleep in it whenever they stayed over. Predictably, she got her way, and even got Cantona to sign it 'To the REAL boss.'

That, however, wasn't the strangest incident that night, not even close. When it came to Cantona's speech, he was handed the microphone and, instead of standing up, he simply leaned forward in his chair. The audience were waiting with bated breath for his words of wisdom and he said,

'Shhhhh, Shhhhh. Can you hear the silence? Thank you.'

And that was it, that's the full transcript of his speech.

Being the ferocious competitor that he is, Fergie made it his mission to ensure his night in 2005 raised the most money. He worked relentlessly to get the key people there on the night; he was amazingly generous, not just financially but also with his time. Every year, we ask the recipient to host a lunch or dinner which we auction off. Such was the phenomenal interest in a meal for five with Fergie on the night that he agreed to host four separate ones. Little wonder that his evening raised in the region of £700,000, a record for Legends of Football. Even now, he still asks if anybody has ever broken it and looks delighted when I tell him it still stands.

Football's generosity is something to behold. José Mourinho was our recipient in 2011 and he flew in from Madrid with his agent, Jorge Mendes, and pretty much all of his backroom staff. Between them, Mourinho and Mendes decided to bid on *every* auction prize, including a Fiat 500 which was up on ramps in the ballroom at the

Grosvenor and that José signed beforehand. I'm not quite sure if the pair knew what they were actually bidding on every time, it was just their way of jousting and raising money but, in the end, José won the car.

A few days later, the phone rings and it's José calling from Madrid. 'I won the car,' he said, 'but I don't want it.' Somewhat taken aback, I said that I knew somebody who would probably buy it, but that I couldn't guarantee José he'd get his money back. 'No, no, you don't understand,' he said. 'I don't want it back, just auction it again for the charity.' Which we did the following year and Alex McLeish's wife Jill snapped it up for about the same money José had paid the year before.

Most of the time, organization for the dinner runs pretty smoothly, and there's been nothing to match the panic of the Cloughie night, although we did think we would have to admit defeat when a hurricane in the Atlantic looked like preventing Pelé from flying in from New York. Thankfully, he'd been in London previously, and we filmed him at the Nordoff Robbins centre in Highgate. There's the greatest player to have ever graced the game, sitting down, playing an array of musical instruments, just trying to help people communicate in a way that makes sense to them. Luckily, the storms subsided, and Pelé was able to join us on the night.

It has to be said, Pelé also did me one of the great turns of my career, albeit inadvertently. I'd got to know him a little, working at the World Cup, where he was with one of his sponsors, and also over the course of the Legends of Football night, so the next time he was in the country, there was a chance our paths would cross.

At this particular time, Louis van Gaal, when he was manager at Manchester United, was giving me a particularly tough time for some reason, scowling at me and being dismissive in pre- and post-match interviews. I was covering United versus Liverpool and had just been on the end of another van Gaal barb when Pelé came into view, walking towards us.

Obviously, Pelé and van Gaal knew each other so the United boss threw his arms wide in greeting. Incredibly, Pelé walked past him, said, 'Geoff, how are you?' and hugged me first before turning back to van Gaal. I'm not sure how much his sponsors were paying him to be in England, but I would have gladly doubled it just for the satisfaction of that moment.

The list of recipients is incredible and includes Alan Shearer, Tony Adams, Steven Gerrard, Frank Lampard, as well as those players who've played 500 or more Premier League games, and most of the 100 Club, who've scored a century of Premier League goals.

I have to admit to gently stitching up David Beckham on his night when it came to the auction. I'd managed to get my hands on an Arsenal shirt signed by all the side who'd won the FA Cup that year, and it was trotting along nicely when I said, 'Hold on, I've just spotted an inscription at the bottom of the shirt. It says, "Happy birthday, Romeo, all my love, Dad." So, any other bidders?' I knew it was both Romeo's birthday that day and he is an Arsenal fan.

And Becks looked at me as if to say, 'You've done me here,' and he *had* to start bidding. Amazingly, the shirt went to ten grand, with Becks leading the way and, although there were a few others willing to go higher, I gave it to

David for being such a good sport. Like Fergie, he agreed to an extra dinner date at the Dorchester and raised £80,000 in the process.

With people like Beckham, you sometimes don't realize the circles in which they move, and their celebrity can still astonish. The night has traditionally been a mix of football and music, as you'd expect, and we've had some great acts like Stereophonics, Roger Daltrey, Mick Hucknall and Russell Watson. For Beckham's night, though, we'd been let down and were scrambling around for a replacement.

David got to hear about it and got in touch. 'I've got a mate who does a bit of comedy,' he said, 'I can ask him to do fifteen minutes of his new stuff if you like?' Erring on the side of caution, I explained it was a big night and, with the greatest respect to David's pal, I didn't want this to be some kind of stopgap. 'Who's your mate?' I asked. 'Oh, Michael McIntyre. I know he'd love to do it.' And McIntyre was brilliant; he did a forty-minute set and brought the house down.

So many people put themselves out for the event that it's difficult to know where to start. Ahead of the night we celebrated the leading goal-scorers in the Premier League. We asked them all for their favourite goal and the resounding winner was Robin van Persie for his amazing volley from Wayne Rooney's pass for Manchester United against Aston Villa. The only problem was that Robin was playing in Turkey at the time, and the flights out of Istanbul made it impossible for him to attend. Well, until David Dein intervened and arranged a private jet to get the former Arsenal striker into London on time. Robin was so grateful; he made a £25,000 donation to Nordoff Robbins.

For me, Legends of Football has become the second biggest part of my working life. I love the purity of it; we make a lot of money through people's generosity, and we give it to a charity that makes a difference. I know because I've seen it with my own eyes, the joy that music therapy brings to those who are suffering in so many ways. I've seen dementia patients who struggle to remember or recognize their own family members, be able to sing their favourite song, word-perfect from beginning to end and, for a few hours, their loved ones have that person back.

In 2017, Brian McLaughlin said he was stepping down as chairman of the organizing committee because he thought it was time for fresh faces. He'd dedicated so much time and effort to get the event off the ground and to build it to what has become, in Fergie's words, 'the best social night on the football calendar'. Brian and I were chatting about his decision when he said, 'I'm not sure you quite get it, Geoff. I'm standing down, but only on the understanding you take over as chairman.' I was honoured, if not a little daunted.

It's become a massive event with an annual turnover of close to a million pounds, and the support I get from two people in particular, financial controller Malgorzata Peal and commercial director Emily Philp, is beyond words. Without them we would be lost. Their dedication and hard work means the event is not only smoothly run but, crucially, continually evolves. Also, like many of our supporters and fantastic committee members both past and present, they really are emotionally invested in the cause.

The Premier League have been amazing supporters from the moment the former chief executive, Richard Scudamore, pledged their backing way back in the early years. Since then, they've provided us with auction prizes like the chance to play at Anfield, Stamford Bridge and the Emirates. Not only that, the Premier League's presence gives us a credibility and a status which people recognize. We can't thank Peta Bistany and Alastair Bennet in particular from the Premier League enough for their constant, tireless support.

It's perhaps no surprise that Alan Curbishley was a great advocate when Brian McLaughlin wrote to all the Premier League managers ahead of our first event. Curbs was the only one to reply. His brother, Bill, has been The Who's manager for many years, and Curbs loved the tie-in between football and music. He phoned Brian before that first dinner and asked if he could bring a couple of guests along. Fine, but who? Only Sir Alex Ferguson and Sir Bobby Robson, who both loved a night out and who have since been our honoured guests over the years. Curbs has been a key figure in establishing our credibility within the footballing world.

There are some other people like Curbs who have been with us from Day One. Miles Jacobson, the irrepressible founder of the computer game, Football Manager. He always has a competition with another great supporter, Richard Bernstein, who works in the City, to see who can sell the most tables and deliver the best auction prizes. A special word for the two Craigs, Adam and David, who, between them, know the world and its dog in football and are always a huge help with getting the great and the good along on the night. It's people like that who are beyond invaluable.

Now, I always share hosting duties, but even that can give you kittens. One year, Kelly Cates was due to be alongside me on the night, but rang me early in the morning, utterly unable to speak. Her voice had gone so badly that it was unrecognizable as Kelly and she was distraught to be letting us down, albeit unavoidably.

It's now around midday on the day of the dinner and I was frantically going through my contacts book, trying to get hold of somebody to fill in for Kelly. I rang Hayley McQueen from Sky.

'Hayley, I'm in the shit, I need your help,' I pleaded.

'OK, what's the event? Where is it and what time do you need me?'

It transpired she was in York but would jump in the car immediately, flung a dress in the back and drive the four hours down the M1 to be in London just before the event started. No script needed, hair and make-up done in record time and on stage as if she'd had weeks to prepare. A magnificent professional and one to whom I will forever be thankful.

There have been a few incidents from the night, though, that beggar belief – and they've usually occurred in the early hours at the after-show party when people have had a chance to 'relax' and possibly cold drinks have been taken.

At the end of one long night, the few of us still surviving had all gathered in the hotel bar. The unlikely group included Wayne Rooney's long-time agent, Paul Stretford, and the singer Aled Jones, plus a few of Aled's friends. Now, Aled was perfectly behaved, but I'm not sure the same could be said of one of his entourage.

Suddenly, one of them took umbrage at something Paul

said and was on his feet, swinging a fair few punches. At first, Paul started laughing, thinking it was all a bit of a joke, but when he got caught on the jaw, the streetfighter in him came roaring to the surface and he landed a couple of looping right-handers himself, giving far better than he was getting off Aled's mate.

Eventually, people jump in and separate the pair, it all calms down and Paul sits back down, remarkably unfazed by events. I can't say the same for Aled. He was in a real state, terrified there would be CCTV footage of the fight, that it would get leaked to the papers and that the headlines would be screaming about the *Songs of Praise* presenter being caught up in a late-night bar brawl after a charity event. I think he could see his choirboy reputation flashing before his eyes.

We calmed him down and packed him off to bed, telling him there was nothing to worry about; nothing would come back on him and that there has been absolutely no damage done. To be fair, Stretty was on the phone first thing in the morning to Aled to make sure there were no hard feelings or lingering recriminations. He was the ultimate professional.

I, on the other hand, saw an opportunity for a little wind-up. At about 11 o'clock the next morning, I woke up, and everything from the previous night came rushing back to me, most notably, Aled's panic-stricken fear that he'd inadvertently been caught up in some kind of shock-horror scandal. I phoned him on a withheld number and, when he answered, I put on my best falsetto and, to the tune of 'Walking in the Air', which he had famously sung in the film *The Snowman*, trilled 'They were fighting in the bar.'

I could hear the horror in his voice. 'WHO IS THIS? WHAT ARE YOU TALKING ABOUT?'

'There were punches being thrown . . .'

'Who is this? Who are you?'

I couldn't keep it up. 'Aled, it's Shreevesie. How are you this morning?'

'You BASTARD. You complete BASTARD. How could you do this to me?'

To paraphrase Sir Alex Ferguson. 'Football and music. Bloody hell.'

11

Closed Grounds, Closed Shop

You could feel it in the air as soon as we arrived at Old Trafford. It wasn't just the sight of the steel barriers and fences being erected around the ground by police and security personnel, there was something tangible about the atmosphere, something that I hadn't experienced since the night in Dublin back in 1995 when England fans rioted.

Sunday 2 May 2021 was the culmination of the most soulless two years of my career. Of course, it was no different for any other person in the country, as Covid-19 destroyed every element of normality and, no, I am incredibly grateful and thankful my life wasn't touched by tragedy. And not for a single moment does anything I experienced register on the same scale as what hundred and thousands of frontline workers endured.

Football, though, operated within weirdly different parameters, as if the reality of a global pandemic was pushed to one side for the sake of ninety minutes. The knock-on effects for the game and – most importantly – the fans were conflated into an outpouring of protest that day in Manchester. The frustration and angst of lockdown, compounded by the rise and swift demise of the European Super League (ESL) had empowered supporters. It felt like thousands of fans who descended on Old Trafford and Manchester city centre that day were swept along by a perfect storm.

Was it understandable? Absolutely. I think we all felt there had to be some kind of outlet or release valve, but that didn't stop it becoming one of the most uncomfortable situations I've ever faced in my thirty-year career.

When I arrived in Manchester much earlier that day, there was already intelligence that United fans were planning a protest against the Glazers. United's proposed participation in the ESL had reignited simmering feelings of discontent, and a high-profile match against Liverpool, another club who had been shamed out of the breakaway by their own fans, was always going to be a target.

From around three hours before the 4.30 p.m. kick-off, United fans were swarming in off Sir Matt Busby Way onto the main Old Trafford concourse and making their way towards a tunnel where United officials and players would normally access the stadium. At the same time, another smaller group was converging on the Lowry Hotel where the United team was preparing for the game. It was clear from all the reports reaching us that there was every intention to get the game called off.

With this in mind, our producer on the day, Jack Hazard, stationed a camera on the top of Hotel Football, which overlooks the ground and, as an editorial team, we discussed how we were going to plan the day to cover every eventuality.

I was reporting, Dave Jones was hosting with Roy Keane, Graeme Souness and Micah Richards in the open-air studio, while Martin Tyler, Gary Neville and Jamie Carragher were commentating. Between us, we have years of experience but, I'd venture to say, none of us had ever been in the situation we faced that day.

In Dublin in 1995, myself and Sky's reporter, Nick Collins, had simply been covering events as England fans tore up the stadium, causing the match with Ireland to be abandoned. At Old Trafford, Sky became a target of fan anger.

Around two hours before kick-off, Carra and I were doing a live cross into *Sky Sports News* from close to the tunnel, talking about the game and the teams and what we could expect from the match – just the general run-of-the-mill game-day discussions. Suddenly, we become aware of shouts coming from the opposite end of the ground as hundreds of fans broke into Old Trafford and began to occupy the pitch.

We had to switch into news reporting mode because events had obviously overtaken the game. At first, I described the protests as peaceful, but it soon became clear there was a much darker edge to it. Supporters were letting off flares, shouting anti-Glazer chants, swinging on the crossbar, ripping up the corner flags. There was an obvious rage and it spilled over towards Sky, as they fired flares towards where Jamie and I were positioned before one fan grabbed a cameraman's tripod and hurled it in our direction.

We carried on reporting for as long as possible but eventually, for our safety and that of the cameramen and sound guys, we moved away from the tunnel and higher up towards a platform where Dave Jones and the studio guests were positioned, while police and security did their best to clear the pitch and usher the protestors out of the stadium. What we didn't know was that a large group had broken away from the main mob and had actually made it down the Old Trafford tunnel, destroying all the Covid protocols set up to protect the players and staff.

When they were discovered, police and security corralled them and, again, sought to get them out of the stadium. But in doing so, they marched them past our platform. Now we were confronted by many of the same people who had been targeting Jamie and me in the first place, and they hurled beer cans in our direction and the fury of fans who were venting in our direction, especially towards Carra, Graeme and Micah for their very obvious Liverpool and Manchester City affiliations.

I have to say, we were all glad of the presence of Roy and Gary on the day, United legends who listened to the protests and immediately had the respect of the fans. Thankfully, they were a calming influence and helped to dilute a confrontation that was threatening to get even further out of hand.

From the moment those fans got down the tunnel, it was clear there was no way the match could now take place. Restrictions within grounds at the time were so tight, and for people outside of the United bubble to break into the Covid 'Red Zone' decimated the rigorous health protocols implemented by the Premier League. That – together with the fact United fans had prevented the team coach from leaving the Lowry – meant the authorities had no option but to postpone the game. Finally, the game was called off at 5.30 p.m., a full hour after it was scheduled to start.

To me, that day summed up a hugely difficult period for the sport as a whole, yet it also served as a full stop. As I said earlier, this had been bubbling because supporters had to endure lockdown and the fact they obviously couldn't go to games. Then they had to face up to the six biggest clubs attempting to destroy the very fabric of English football with their breakaway, and suddenly there was a seemingly existential threat to the very thing that so many millions of people hold dear, and they rose up.

To see the dominoes falling as each club realized just what a massive mistake they'd made was incredibly satisfying. Fan and public outrage forced them to back-pedal spectacularly, and no number of conciliatory videos from the other side of the Atlantic could make up for their huge misstep.

The day the story broke, we were covering Manchester United versus Burnley on *Super Sunday* but the only story of the day was the Super League. Producer Matt Roberts played an absolute blinder that day. Coverage of the game didn't matter quite so much; all that anybody wanted to talk about was the ramifications of a breakaway, so we devoted half-time and post-match to covering that.

Gary Neville was excellent, I have to say, crystallizing what all fans thought in a passionate but thoughtful way. He knew a supporter rebellion, properly aligned, could defeat the clubs. And he was right.

Fan protest utterly derailed the ESL in the space of six

days, and humiliated billionaire owners, so a logical step was to again gather on the streets in order that their voices were heard. Honestly, I couldn't blame the supporters at Old Trafford because they'd been utterly disrespected by the club's hierarchy, but some of their actions were illegal and wrong. From a journalistic perspective, to be at the heart of the story on the ground was obviously important; however, somebody could have been seriously injured, or worse.

There was so much about those two years or so from March 2020 that none of us ever want to repeat.

The early days of the pandemic saw an absolute re-invention of the way that I, and many others at Sky, had worked for decades. I hesitate to use the word 'exciting', because it seems so trite when put in the context of what others had to suffer and endure, but the restrictions imposed on us led to a pioneering spirit which saw us create programmes in a completely new way.

Technology was obviously the key and a piece of kit called V-Mix suddenly opened all kinds of doors. Football may have gone into hibernation, but V-Mix allowed us to create programmes from our homes alongside Zoom, which had previously been seen as a poor substitute for having a guest in a studio or in front of a camera, suddenly becoming our go-to tool.

It was decided that we would have the daily *Football Show*, which Dave Jones and Kelly Cates mainly hosted, although I did a few. In my normal day job, the biggest challenge I would normally face is when a groundsman decides to unex-pectedly turn on the sprinklers and I have to beat a hasty retreat, or there's a rogue tannoy announcement. Now we had to worry about an Amazon delivery, the dog inadvertently gatecrashing a broadcast, the next-door neighbour mowing the lawn or a police siren.

We were doing the jobs that it normally takes ten people to do. All presenters and reporters got sent a pack through, consisting of lights, your own make-up kit, and all the paraphernalia we take for granted when preparing a programme. There was no talkback in your ear; all the directions came through by text from the director, and we were all at the mercy of the blessed Wi-Fi signal.

It was flying by the seat of your pants, but there was also a true camaraderie amongst the team that we were meeting all the obstacles head-on and, in a tiny way, triumphing. I have to pay tribute to the likes of Billy McGinty, Jack Hazard, Matt Roberts and Sam Mills, people behind the scenes who don't normally get public recognition but who absolutely drove our coverage. They were remarkable in terms of the innovation they brought to the situation.

And football bought into what Sky was attempting. I think managers and players were searching for their own small piece of normalcy, and if that meant doing an interview or joining a discussion, then they were up for it even if, on the odd occasion, things went awry, like Claudio Ranieri being interviewed by Kelly when suddenly his wife joined from another room because she had somehow joined his Zoom call. Or Graeme Souness with his AirPods in upside down because that was the only way they'd fit his ears!

It was a brilliant effort from so many people to provide some light relief. Of course, it's largely meaningless when you put it in the context of people losing their lives, their loved ones or their incomes but, like everybody in the country, we were just trying to find a way through the very best we could.

I also continued to host *The Debate* through part of lockdown, a show of which I'm incredibly proud. To be able to get on hugely relevant and interesting guests simply to discuss and talk through the biggest issues of the day was invigorating, challenging and incredibly satisfying. The calibre of guests we had on was testament to the show's standing. People like Roy Hodgson, Karren Brady, Craig Bellamy and Danny Murphy all took part, and to give people like Sol Campbell a platform to discuss his belief he was not getting managerial jobs simply because of the colour of his skin felt incredibly important. Unfortunately, lockdown meant we couldn't continue to show *The Debate* because you really do need the guests to be in the same room. Debate in and around football and all its issues is so fulfilling. If ever there was a chance to bring it back, I'd love to be involved again.

The mood changed when we went back to covering matches a few months later; that's when the soullessness really kicked in. Players and managers, quite rightly, wondered exactly why they were being treated as guinea pigs while the rest of society was still locked down, and I understood exactly why they felt like they were part of some huge experiment. Why, when the rest of the country could only meet people within their own bubble, were players expected to physically challenge each other all over the pitch, but then get changed in different parts of the ground? The validity of these questions was difficult to counter.

The whole experience of going to games was shorn of any human contact because of the stringent restrictions. Where I might travel to a game with somebody, be it a studio guest or co-commentator or on the train, now I drove on my own. There was no ability to go and get something to eat or drink, no chance to chat with journalistic colleagues, no feeling of humanity in anything we were doing.

Obviously, we were all masked up and had to stay two metres apart. The intimacy that comes from being a mere arm's length away from the person you're interviewing is destroyed because, other than struggling to hear what people say, you also can't gauge their mood from their facial expressions. It felt fake and anodyne.

I hated the solitary experience. By nature, I'm gregarious and love other people's company, the conversation, the jokes, the laughs; that sense of community within football. Now we were stripped of everything that forms part of the job. What it did do, though, was give me a deep-seated respect for the team on the ground that puts our coverage together. For once, I was getting an insight into their normal way of life: being outside in the cold for hours on end, not having the opportunity to sit in a warm press lounge, having to be out there three hours before kick-off and still working three hours after the final whistle. Suddenly, I had an inkling of what they have to put up with all the time. Nobody is a hero for simply putting on a television programme, but these people have my absolute respect.

The restrictions also created difficulties, not so much when the matches were played behind closed doors – that was just a matter of putting up with masks and doing your best to create as much of a bond between you and the manager or player as possible. It was when some fans were allowed back into the ground, and we were still doing interviews two metres apart.

That caused a misunderstanding with Jürgen Klopp and led to a very spiky interview. He was explaining something about the Liverpool defence, and I was straining to hear him and I kind of screwed my eyes up so I could concentrate on exactly what point he was trying to make. He obviously saw something different and said, 'Oh, I see from your face you don't believe what I'm saying?' Nothing could have been further from the truth – I simply couldn't hear him.

The same with Arsenal's Emile Smith Rowe after he scored in the North London derby. At one stage, he said how scoring against Tottenham and Arsenal winning was the highlight of his career, and that nothing had ever come close to matching the feeling. I, however, was totally oblivious, because the crowd noise drowned out the conversation. It's only through sheer chance that my follow-up question wasn't along the lines of 'How good does this feel?' and major embarrassment. I got lucky.

The sheer volume of games after 17 June through to the end of the season was astonishing – and every one of the ninety-two was covered live by Sky, the BBC or Amazon. It was a Herculean task. There were some incredible moments, too, especially when Liverpool won their first title for thirty years. I take my hat off to everybody at Anfield for the way they delivered on the night Jordan Henderson lifted the Premier League trophy, because it must have been devastating not to celebrate in front of your fans, but the spectacle Liverpool put on was a credit to the club. It was like a rock concert.

But the thing driving everybody was the prospect of just getting through to the end of the season and being able to start afresh with fans back in the ground and all the Covid protocols lifted. Those first few games when fans were allowed in was like standing on an African plain when the drought breaks, and the rain reinvigorates everything it touches. We thought we were through the worst of it, that life would be normal again before too long.

How sadly mistaken we were.

12

The Shreeves A–Z

A is for ADVICE

Just before Wes Morgan goes out to receive the Premier League trophy, I pull him aside to tell a cautionary tale. One particular captain, just before he hoists a piece of silverware, plants a kiss on it and says, 'You fucking beauty!' You can lip-read every word, so it is rarely shown. Wes nods sagely and then, proudly and professionally, goes on to perform probably the most popular Premier League trophy lift of all time.

B is for BERGKAMP

Or, put another way, the finest player to have graced the Premier League. Well, at least in my opinion. In terms of his technical ability and artistry, he was the closest thing to Johan Cruyff that I've seen.

On the twentieth anniversary of his astonishing goal against Newcastle in 2002, there was still huge debate as to whether he had meant it. The man himself had given me his answer some years before when I was invited to Amsterdam for the launch of his book, *Stillness and Speed*.

He told me football is like trigonometry; that there are always patterns and it's not about reacting, it's about predicting what will happen. A little hesitantly, I asked whether he understood when people suggested there was luck involved in that particular goal and, shattering all my illusions, he said there was luck involved. But he then went on to explain.

'When I showed for the ball, I wanted it on my right foot, but Robert Pires fired it in on my left, so that was the first bit of luck. Then, I gambled that Nikos Dabizas was touch-tight, so that was my second piece of luck, but everything else? I knew exactly what I was doing.'

A one hundred per cent genius.

C is for COCK-UPS

Throughout my broadcasting career, I have not only established but maintained a distinctively unimpressive track record when it comes to mangling my words. Names, places, even football clubs have all, at various times, been strangled, leaving viewers wondering what this gabbling fool is on about.

Nicolas Anelka should be pretty straightforward, you would have thought, but I managed to announce him as 'Nicolas Fannelka'. And when the Leeds United head groundsman, Norman Southernwood, performed heroics in getting a game on despite a torrential downpour, it seemed right to mention him in dispatches for his efforts. Unfortunately, he became Northerly Southerly in the process.

Even Romelu Lukaku didn't escape during one particularly shaky team news bulletin, when the then Everton striker became 'Romelu Lukakkaka', as if I was auditioning for the Vic Reeves role on *Shooting Stars* introducing Ulrikakaka Jonsson.

Sam Allardyce worked wonders at Bolton Wanderers and brought some incredible players to the club, the pinnacle being the arrival of World Cup winner, Youri Djorkaeff, in the Premier League. This was European footballing royalty, one of the most familiar faces, let alone names, on the continent. Not to me though, as I called him Djorki Yourieff live on *Soccer AM*.

Struggling to retain my composure after this horrendous gaffe, I thought I'd got away with it until I sensed a presence to my right as somebody emerged from the players' tunnel. It was Djorkaeff himself, wearing a look of utter bemusement and disdain. 'Why can't you say my name properly? Don't you know who I am?' he not unreasonably enquired as I verbally tap-danced spectacularly and tried to joke my way out of my dreadful error, stumbling and falling with every stuttering word.

Mercifully my torture was ended by a huge roar of laughter from behind me and the arrival of Big Sam, who'd witnessed my faux pas and had sent out Youri to wind me up. Bastard!

D is for DEPARTURE

If you have got this far in the book, you'll have seen Andy Gray and Richard Keys played a significant part in the first two decades of Sky's coverage. I will always be grateful for all the help that they gave me.

E is for ENGLAND

Sadly, my first experience of covering England in the 1990 World Cup was my international highlight for decades. So many false dawns, so many missed opportunities, so many subsequent disappointments and, for years, nothing matched the memories of Italia '90.

There have been some bright spots along the way, like the night in Munich when England beat Germany 5-1 in 2001. I remember positioning David Beckham for an interview with the scoreboard in the background and him just looking over his shoulder as if he still couldn't quite believe it.

The trips covering the games have been about the best thing, travelling the world with so many great colleagues, journalists and friends, feeling like you're in a privileged club. In Russia and then the Euro's, Gareth Southgate and the boys brought a new sense of optimism and I would love to think an England tournament win will happen in Qatar to give us all something to write home about in my lifetime.

F is for FULHAM

Well, more specifically, Craven Cottage, by a country mile my favourite football ground in England. I know it's limited in terms of numbers and facilities, but its sheer antiquated charm is impossible to beat.

Mick Luckhurst was bringing some American clients to a game once and he rang me to ask where he should take them. He was willing to spend fortunes because it was an important account and worth digging deep to get the very best hospitality.

My advice was to get tickets for a Fulham home game, have a wander down the Thames, stop at a couple of the local pubs and then stroll through Bishop's Park to the ground. He rang me the next day and said he would have paid twenty times what it cost for such a wonderfully traditional event that the Americans absolutely loved.

G is for GREATEST

I've had this list on my whiteboard in my office for days and I've been dreading this one. Because how do you whittle down so many fantastic games and goals over thirty-plus years? It's impossible, and if you ask me the same question in a year's time, I'd probably give you a completely different answer.

The best goals I've seen? Thierry Henry has a couple, his flick up and volley past Fabien Barthez and the goal he scored against Liverpool in the Invincibles season when he seemingly scorched past half a dozen players on his way to a hat-trick.

Tony Yeboah's thunderbolt against Liverpool in 1995, when he smashed it home from thirty yards, and the Elland Road bar was rattling for days afterwards. The technique involved in Mateo Kovačić's astonishing volley versus Liverpool, and Wayne Rooney's overhead in the Manchester derby will always be right up there. Shearer's volley against Everton.

That's five, but I could go on for a month and still not recall them all.

As for matches I've covered; well, three Champions League finals stick out: Manchester United for the Treble in the Nou Camp in 1999, Liverpool in Istanbul and Chelsea sticking it to Bayern Munich in their own back yard all have a place in my heart.

But for sheer drama and passion, the first 4-3 between Liverpool and Newcastle and the abiding memory of Kevin Keegan slumped over the advertising hoardings in front of the away team dugout takes some beating.

H is for HOULLIER and HARFORD

I couldn't possibly ignore either Gérard Houllier or Ray Harford, two men I miss hugely. Gérard was just one of the most generous people I have ever met in the game, who would go out of his way to be helpful – ridiculously so at times. He would never allow me to get a taxi in Paris and would always send a driver to pick me up from the airport. Then we would be welcome in his beautiful apartment next to Roland Garros where we would always film the interview, never a hotel.

He got Champions League final tickets for a friend of

mine but, unfortunately, those tickets got misplaced. Even though Gérard was very unwell at the time, he insisted on helping to sort out the problem and resolved the issue. That was the mark of the man.

He was such a paternal figure to so many of the Liverpool players, especially the younger ones like Steven Gerrard who broke into the squad under Gérard. When we paid tribute to Stevie at Legends of Football, Gérard gave a speech I remember to this day. He said, 'I told Stevie when he was younger that, yes, I knew he liked going out to nightclubs but, if he took my advice, when he retired, he would be successful enough to OWN nightclubs.'

Ray Harford was an absolute gem. Those that didn't know him may have perhaps thought he was a little dour, but they missed one of the funniest guys you could wish to meet.

I first got to know him when he was manager of Blackburn and he refused to do an interview for Sky. Richard Keys told the viewers that we wanted to talk to Ray but that Ray didn't want to talk to Sky.

I was the floor manager and Ray came over to me and said, 'Sky have just said I wouldn't do an interview.' 'Well, you wouldn't,' I replied. 'Right, let's do one now,' he said, and we proceeded to do one on the spot. When we'd finished, he said, 'Right, well what do you think now?' 'I think you were better when you didn't do it!' He roared with laughter and that was the start of a long friendship.

He was a studio guest many times and always brought something different to the analysis. Alan Shearer talks about what a fantastic coach he was and a vital ingredient in Blackburn's title-winning season. They did a finishing

drill with the ball crossed for the strikers to head home.
Ray would say, 'If the cross is good enough, you don't have
to put power on the ball, just nod and say, "Good morning"
to the football.' When he passed away it meant a lot to us
at Sky when his family got in touch to say how much the
tribute we had paid to him moved them.

I is for ISTANBUL

To have great broadcasts, you need great games. Liverpool's
triumph in Istanbul will go down as one of the greatest.

Sky were very fortunate that night: we won the toss with
the other broadcasters to go first with our interviews, so
captured the immediate rapture of the occasion with the
players barely able to comprehend what they'd achieved.
I'd been on a journey to where it all began for Jerzy Dudek
starting his career in Poland for a mining works team, only
for him to achieve immortality that night with his penalty
shoot-out saves.

It was an astonishing, amazing memory, and not one of
us on the Sky team minded that we didn't get back to our
hotel until 7 a.m. the next morning.

Istanbul is also memorable for a huge row in the tunnel
between England and Turkey players, which almost caused
an international incident in 2003. To this day, I'm not sure
what sparked it, but I was in the tunnel area and all I
could see was a mass of bodies piling into each other, with
Emile Heskey obviously hugely aggrieved at something that
had been said or done.

We couldn't film, but I was able to surreptitiously report
live from the scene and that was enough for me to be

called by the FA's solicitors to give evidence after UEFA charged both associations. I've still got a copy of my statement.

J is for JAMIE CARRAGHER

It was absolutely no surprise that he became an excellent pundit, given he's a complete football obsessive. I remember interviewing him in his playing days and asking if it was true that, on a Sunday off, he'd watch *Sunday Supplement*, followed by *Goals on Sunday*, then an EFL game, the two *Super Sunday* matches and then coverage of an Italian game and finally a Spanish match from La Liga?

'No, that's not true,' he said. 'I don't always watch the Spanish game.'

K is for KEVIN KEEGAN

Most people will remember Kevin for his 'I would love it' rant but, for me, I have fond memories of his marvellous, heart-on-the-sleeve, joyous approach to the game. Yes, he was flawed as a manager, but his principles were brilliant: attack, attack, attack.

When he got the England job, I went to interview him at the FA's old Lancaster Gate headquarters. We'd set up the cameras and the lights and started the interview when Kevin talked about how his dad, who had passed, would be so proud. The moment he mentioned his dad, all the bulbs on the lights popped.

Not a problem, we simply re-set and began the interview again, with Kevin repeating the story about his dad. Again, the moment his dad was mentioned, all the lights went again. All a bit too spooky, so we moved on.

I was also in the Wembley tunnel in 2001 on the day he quit the England job. It was the last ever game at the Twin Towers, we'd lost 1-0 to Germany in the pouring rain and Kevin had walked off the pitch a broken man. Through a window, I could see him deep in conversation with FA chiefs and it was clear there was something happening, even though all the players were tight-lipped as they left the dressing room.

Sensing there was something seismic in the offing, the producer told transmission we simply had to stay on air, and we were rewarded when Sky broke the news an hour or so later that Kevin had quit.

L is for JENS LEHMANN

Lots of people, quite rightly, have an image of Jens as a – frankly – mad German, with all the histrionics, play-acting and arguments that he seemed to embody for ninety minutes of a match. I shared that belief until Arsenal played a game against Liverpool and he was absolutely outstanding, even in a defeat. So impressive was his performance that he was voted man-of-the-match which, I have to say, is less frequent for a player from the losing side.

We put in an interview request but were told by the Arsenal media team that he wasn't interested in either collecting his MotM champagne or doing an interview, promptly underlining my perception of him.

I was at the Arsenal training ground the following week

so I thought I'd take along the champagne and give it to him during the interview that he had agreed to.

We started the interview and I said, 'Jens, you were a man-of-the-match last week, but you chose not to do the interview, so I've brought you the bottle anyway.'

And his reply took me aback and immediately made me reconsider my opinion of him. 'First,' he said 'I've got to apologize to both you and the sponsors for not conducting the interview last week, and I will explain why. I actually haven't had that many awards, certainly not in this country, so I'm extremely grateful and I'm extremely proud to receive this.

'But the truth is, we had just lost in the last minute at Anfield and the team were deflated, we were so, so flat. I just felt that for me to go out and receive an individual reward and then carry it onto the coach would have looked so arrogant and so self-centred. I couldn't do it. So, I hope you understand my thought process and once again, I apologize to you, but thank you very, very much indeed for recognizing my performance.'

He couldn't have been more charming, articulate, or sensitive, and rotated my opinion of him a full 180 degrees.

M is for MUTINY

It was obvious from the moment Carlos Tevez started warming up on the touchline in Munich's Olympic Stadium that something was badly wrong between him and the Manchester City boss, Roberto Mancini. The tension between them on that night in 2011 was palpable.

When Tevez sat down and was then told to start warming

up again by Mancini, he flatly refused, apparently claiming he was ready to go on and didn't need to warm up any further. To Mancini, this was mutiny. I broke the story from my position next to the dug out.

Afterwards, it was clear the Italian was still apoplectic with rage, but even I wasn't prepared for how far he was willing to go in his interview. According to him, Tevez had refused to play, would never pull on a City shirt while Mancini was still the manager and he had no intention of back-tracking on those sentiments. We then got a brilliant exclusive when I managed to follow that up with words from Tevez through a translator, who absolutely denied he'd refused to play.

It was a story that ran for weeks and a decent night's work to get all the elements of the tale ahead of everybody else.

N is for GARY NEVILLE

I'm convinced Gary doesn't sleep at night; he reboots, like a computer. Because no mere mortal can have that many ideas fizzing through his brain at the same time, surviving on about four hours' kip. There is so much energy to him, so many ideas, plans and businesses that it's impossible to keep up with him at times.

To be honest, I didn't do too many interviews with him as a player, although he does credit me with being the person who brought him to Sky. When I said to him that, doing both punditry or commentary, you need light and shade he said, 'Don't worry, Geoff, I'll bring plenty of shade!' One of the first times our paths crossed was a slightly inauspicious introduction. Manchester United were playing Coventry City at Highfield Road and had fallen behind in the first half to a hotly disputed goal, with Sir Alex and all the United players convinced it was offside.

At the break, I was in the tunnel and began walking back to the pitch when I passed the United dressing room, where the door was open and Fergie and all the players were silently waiting to go back out. 'Was it offside?' 'No,' I replied.

'Who was keeping them onside then?'

'Gary Neville.'

As the United players made their way up the tunnel, Gary passed me and said, 'Thanks for that,' accompanied by an ironic smile.

O is for OLYMPICS

Not because I believe football should be in the Olympics – because I don't. I wouldn't cross the road to watch a match at the Games. But when Sky asked me to take part in their Scholar Scheme, I was intrigued.

Basically, you're paired with a young athlete in a field in which you have some expertise, so Annabel Croft was paired with a young tennis player, Johnny Nelson a boxer and so on. When it came to me, Sky obviously studied my ripped physique and stunning athleticism and promptly paired me with . . . a gymnast!

Sam Oldham and I got on famously over the three year term in which we worked together. It's all about life experience, and the kind of advice sportsmen and -women are looking for outside of their parents or their coach, perhaps just coping methods and mentoring on how to deal with certain facets that come with having to contend with being a high-performing athlete.

When Sky asked if I would consider a second term, I jumped at the opportunity. This time I was paired with a sprinter, Imani-Lara Lansiquot, and again, we got on like a house on fire. We just chat, there's no programme. I tend to just offer advice I've picked up from talking to top footballers. It's just a thought process, a word here or there. To be honest, I have learned a great deal from Imani too.

I can't remember being as nervous as I was while watching Imani when she was part of the Great Britain 4 × 100-metre team that won bronze at the Tokyo Games. I was thrilled for her because I knew how much hard work, both physical and mental, she had put in.

P is for PRANKS

Like any industry, there are the usual wind-ups. In television, when you're asked for a voice level, you just mouth the words and that sends the guys into a state of panic. But there are times when you go too far.

I was in Newcastle ahead of a game, just sitting in the lunch truck, having a cuppa and a sandwich, when I spotted Sky's then north-east man, David Craig, rehearsing a piece to camera. It was obviously just a scene-setter so I decided to have a bit of fun and leaned out of the window, and shouted all sorts of nonsense at my pal, trying to put him off.

Ten minutes later, Craigy joined me in the lunch truck.

'Sorry about that, pal,' I said, 'but I couldn't resist that. Did you re-record it OK?' Craigy looked puzzled. 'What do you mean?' he asked. 'You know, that pre-record you were doing.' 'You've lost me, mate, that was live.'

My blood just ran cold. In a state of absolute panic, I rang Duncan East, our presentation director, who confirmed that, for whatever reason, the mic hadn't picked up a word I'd said. Otherwise, I could have been on my way to the job centre.

Q is for QUESTIONS

The lifeblood of my job. How to structure a question, the tone you use, when that question comes in an interview. Do you go in hard or hold back without soft-soaping your subject? Never lose sight of who you are asking the question for – it's never other journalists, it's always the audience.

I live by the old maxim that the most important thing about a question is the answer.

R is for REDKNAPP

Jamie Redknapp is by far the best-dressed person I know, who is immaculate every second of the day, the kind of bloke who can get out of a bath without making a puddle. Not only does he look perfect in anything he puts on, but I've also never seen anybody hang a suit like he does. It looks like it's just come from the factory when he's finished.

There was a battle for his services when he decided to

retire, with both Sky and the BBC making a huge play for him. I remember going to his house to convince him to join us and telling him that, at the BBC, he'd be the man on the end of the line of famous faces, whereas at Sky we'd make him a much more central figure, which is exactly how it has worked out.

The only time I've ever seen him look slightly less than cool is when Les Ferdinand offered us both a lift back from an FA Cup final in Cardiff in his helicopter. I knew Les was a qualified pilot, but I didn't for a moment imagine he'd flown down. The thought of a forty-five-minute flight back from Wales instead of a five-hour slog down the M4 was enough to convince Jamie and me that we'd be quids in with Les.

We arrived at the airfield and walked past all these beautiful private jets and gleaming helicopters, until we got to end of the line and there stood what I can only describe as Budgie's little brother. It looked barely big enough for Les, let alone the three of us. However, undaunted, we clambered in. Les went through all the usual pre-flight checks and we were up and away, heading east towards London.

But before we could make it very far, the weather started closing in and the horizon was filled with a cloud of deepest purple, the kind you see in cartoons with lightning flashing out of it. It's fair to say, the mood of the two passengers became somewhat nervous. In fact, we were terrified.

So bad were the conditions that, when Les contacted air traffic control, he was offered a landing slot at RAF Brize Norton in Oxfordshire. Normally, that's off limits to civilian aircraft but did Les want to take the slot? Before he could say a word, Jamie and I were screaming, 'YES, YES, JUST FUCKING LAND!'

Dropped off in the middle of rural Oxfordshire, we then all had to get cars for the rest of the journey, and I arrived back in St Albans about six hours later and definitely a few pounds lighter.

S is for SOUEY

Graeme Souness, what a man. He's done it all in the game; world-class player who won everything with Liverpool, a successful transition to life in Italy, hugely influential manager who changed the face of Scottish football and then took on the biggest challenges at Anfield, Newcastle and of course, famously, Galatasaray.

Wonderful orator with those beautifully rounded vowels and, to the outside world, as tough as teak. To those that know him, though, he's a softie when it comes to friends in trouble or animals. I felt so desperately sorry when Graeme lost his great friend, Michael Robinson, during the pandemic. The pair were so close, and he gave an incredibly moving tribute.

T is for TEDDY SHERINGHAM

Nobody revelled in the atmosphere of a North London derby more than Teddy. He loved sticking it to the Arsenal fans and they, in turn, gave him dog's abuse. Even when he went to Manchester United, the Gooners were still vicious, especially when his trophy cabinet wasn't exactly as full as he might have expected from his early days at

Old Trafford. I know their chant grated on him, 'Oh, Teddy, Teddy, he went to Man United and he won fuck all.'

So at the start of the 1999–2000 season, after United had won the Treble, Sky were covering Arsenal versus United at Highbury and I saw Teddy before he came out to warm up. 'Watch this,' he said, 'I'm going to ram it back down their throats.' So when he went out, he deliberately ran in front of the Arsenal fans and held up three fingers to his chest.

Unfortunately for Teddy, his three medals hardly deterred the Gunners faithful and, as quick as a flash, they shouted, 'Oh, Teddy, Teddy, he went to Man United and he's still a c***.'

Give him his due, as he came back down the tunnel, he was roaring with laughter. He said, 'Fair play, fair play, that's absolutely brilliant.'

U is for UEFA

Where do I start with UEFA? I think the thing that irritates me most – amongst many others, it has to be said – is their constant tampering with the format of the Champions League. It's a spectacular competition, but will be absolutely destroyed by this determination to pander to the biggest, richest clubs every step of the way. It was these clubs that tried to kill off the Champions League with their breakaway plans, but UEFA are still toadying up to them.

Places in the competition for those clubs with a so-called heritage: a disgrace. Why do they think that bigger is better? Keep it special; don't muck around with something that already works brilliantly.

V is for VAR

I'm coming off my long run for this one. The problem is people expect VAR to solve every argument in football and to be 100 per cent conclusive, which is just not possible the moment you invite a secondary opinion. VAR has taken away the power of the referees, who in turn referee differently because they now have an insurance policy, but who can blame them?

It was supposed to rid the game of obvious errors like the Thierry Henry handball for France against the Republic of Ireland. Instead, it's being used for minute decisions that are destroying the way we see the game.

The biggest indictment of VAR is that it has sapped any last vestige of fun from what should be the greatest pleasure for any player – scoring a goal. We spoke to Michail Antonio who used to be known for his glorious celebrations like The Worm, and asked why his response to scoring now seemed relatively muted. No point in celebrating like that any more, he said; not when it can be ruled out by VAR for the width of your shirt and then you look stupid. If the powers that be can't see that scoring a goal is no longer a cause for immediate celebration then we really do have a problem.

And then there's the fans. They are the only people who've actually paid to be in the ground, yet they're the ones who are the last to know what's happening. They haven't got a clue. It's not suspense, it's a diabolical liberty they are being treated so shabbily, and it's an egregious insult.

At Sky, we've always said that watching our games should be the second-best experience you can get, because it's never going to beat actually being in the crowd, but now the viewer at home is being given a better experience than those in the stadium, and that cannot be right. Instead, the fans are being treated with disdain. Let them see what's happening, mic up all concerned and take a leaf out of rugby's book.

W is for WILKINS

Never Butch, always Razor, I miss Ray Wilkins to this day. I miss the cheery response to the question: how are you, mate? 'Dangerously well, fella, dangerously well.' I miss his smile, his lovely turn of phrase and his sheer class.

Look at the clubs he played for: Chelsea, Manchester United, Milan, PSG. That's a list of European royalty. You don't play for those clubs without being a top class player. He so rarely gave the ball away. As Ray would rightly point out, he thought it was much easier playing the game with the ball rather than the opposition having it. Never waste possession. Growing up, my favourite goal in *The Big Match* opening titles was one of his twenty-five yarders crashing in off the crossbar at Stamford Bridge.

The day he died, I was due to present *The Debate*. It was incredibly difficult to compose myself because his death left a huge hole. I know he had his well-documented problems towards the end of his life, but he was taken far, far too young.

He had a famously dry sense of humour, delivered in dead-pan posh Cockney tones. Travelling to a game one day, one of our colleagues in the car was suffering from a flatulence problem which was causing us no end of disgust.

Finally, after yet another explosion, Razor turned to me and said, 'Geoffrey, would you do me a favour? Could you punch me in the face and break my nose, fella?'

Miss you, fella.

X is for X-RATED

Like all broadcasters, Sky never show replays of bad injuries. The minute we know it's serious, we pan away, because there will always be family or friends of the victim watching and there's no way we want to do anything that's going to make them feel any worse than they obviously do.

When Arsenal's Eduardo suffered an horrific injury against Birmingham City, our VT truck immediately downloaded every angle of the incident and burnt it onto a CD as quickly as possible. I then took it to the Arsenal physio, Gary Lewin, so he could see exactly how the injury and the break had occurred, where the impact was, and anything else that might be able to assist Eduardo in his recovery and rehab.

Equally X-rated was the sight of Alan Shearer's testicles. He was covering an England game for us in South Africa, but the day before he flew, Robert Huth had trod on his groin when Newcastle played Chelsea. By the time he'd arrived in Durban, his bollocks had swollen to elephantine-size and were black as night – and still he insisted on showing them to me.

Thanks for that, Al.

Y is for YOU'LL NEVER SEE . . .

Martin Tyler's iconic line to describe Sergio Agüero's astonishing last-second goal to win the title for Manchester City. 'Agüerooooo! I swear you'll never see anything like this again, drink it all in.' Brilliant words to perfectly sum up a moment that encapsulates what is so wonderful about football. It was an astonishing turnaround in fortunes with match director Tony Mills capturing the agony and anguish on the faces of the City supporters followed by Martin's totally spontaneous spine-tingling commentary. Undoubtedly an iconic moment in football and Sky's football coverage.

Z is for ZURAB KHIZANISHVILI

I can only try to convey the sheer terror that gripped me night and day for a full week when in, October 2005, we were going to cover Blackburn Rovers versus Birmingham City and I'm due to do team news. As I have stated previously, I can mess up the simplest of names so when a complicated one started looming, panic set in early.

I thought I had my 'get out of jail free' card when, on the Saturday before the game we were covering, Blackburn's Georgian defender, Zurab Khizanishvili, was sent off against Liverpool. My first reaction was (and this is nothing personal, Zurab), thank God for that, as at least now I won't have to mention him. That minor relief was short-lived when Blackburn decided to appeal the decision, and now I was faced with the very real prospect of getting my tongue around his name.

Every scenario played out in my head. Could I get away

with, 'Same starting eleven as Anfield, which means Bellamy and Dickov up top'? Really poor, I know, but at least it was a way out. To compound matters, I'm told we won't actually discover the result of the appeal until the day of the game. Now there's no escaping it, Mr K is going to be the story of the day.

Over and over I practise it, but the only difference between me and the captain of the *Titanic* is that I know I'm going to hit an iceberg seventy-two hours before it even looms into view. I call all my commentator pals and get the exact phonetic breakdown and, for three days, all I'm repeating to myself is KHIZ-AN-ISH-VILI.

Come the day of the match, Richard Keys tees me up and throws live to me, 'Geoff, Blackburn Rovers were due to hear from the FA this morning, what can you tell us?'

Coolly and calmly, I start with, 'It's good news for Rovers, Richard, Zurab Khizanishvili . . .' Yes, get in! Absolutely nailed it! Perhaps I've got distant Georgian roots, so perfectly did I pronounce his name, his mum couldn't have said it any better.

Unfortunately, that was immediately followed by, 'has had his red turd over carded.'

13

2021/2022
End of Season Diary

Friday 1 April

The World Cup draw takes place in Qatar for the tournament in November. I'll be covering it for the American channel, Fox Sports, and it feels like April Fool's Day when England are drawn with the USA in Group B. The banter starts between me and my US World Cup colleagues. I tell them I am more worried about Canada in the later stages – which goes down really well.

Sunday 3 April

Tottenham thrash Newcastle 5-1 to boost their Champions League chances. Unusually, Harry Kane doesn't score, but it's enjoyable to interview different players post-match so I grab Ben Davies and Matt Doherty. Kane is important that day, though, as he signs a personal message on a shirt for me which has raised an incredible £10,000 at a charity auction. Like virtually every player, Harry is a good guy when it comes to charities and will help out wherever possible.

Monday 4 April

Ahead of Crystal Palace versus Arsenal, I pop into the Selhurst Park boardroom to see chairman Steve Parish. He's quite rightly seething about UEFA's proposal to give the FA Cup winners a place in the Champions League, as long as they have history in the competition. Steve introduces me to Sir Keir Starmer, leader of the Labour Party and a staunch Arsenal fan. He says he's really worried about the left but it's not politics on his mind. Kieran Tierney, the Arsenal left back, is unexpectedly absent with an injury. He's not wrong, Arsenal are walloped 3-0 with Nuno Tavares, Tierney's replacement, hooked at half-time.

Thursday 7 April

Cut short my brother Graham's sixtieth birthday celebrations to travel to Liverpool for an early morning interview the next day with Jürgen Klopp and then Mo Salah. On the train I sit next to Jamie Carragher, Steven Gerrard, Frank Lampard, Rafa Benítez, Wayne Rooney, Mikel Arteta and many more, courtesy of impressionist, Darren Farley, who is a mad Liverpool fan. Tells me he's confident for the potential title deciding game away to Manchester City on Sunday.

Friday 8 April

Talk to Jürgen Klopp, discussing the sheer brilliance of these two teams and how they bring out the best in each other. He is genuinely astonished when I tell him that, since the start of the 2018/19 season, their respective points totals are City 338 and Liverpool 337 – just the one-point difference. He's relaxed and calm ahead of a huge game and Salah confirms there is no update on his contract situation. Despite Egypt missing out on World Cup qualification after the heartbreak of a penalty shoot-out defeat, Salah remains upbeat. He's one of those who, when given time and space to talk, is incredibly warm and engaging.

Sunday 10 April

To the Etihad for Manchester City v Liverpool and you know it's a massive game when the number of foreign broadcasters on site is triple the normal contingent. I bump into Robbie Mustoe, Robbie Earle, Nigel de Jong, Joleon Lescott, Michael Owen and Yaya Touré who are all working for various TV stations. City's in-house channel save their best two guests until last as I hear behind me the intro-duction of Ali Benarbia and Noel Gallagher – there's two names you would never expect in the same sentence. An intense, epic 2-2 draw leaves both managers with mixed feelings, neither delighted nor upset at the result.

Wednesday 13 April

Welcome Gareth Southgate to Nordoff Robbins London headquarters and show him around. As one of our recipients alongside Ellen White at October's dinner in their honour, he's keen to understand exactly how music therapy can help people. He sits in on a session with a young lad called William who unfortunately suffers from numerous conditions. Gareth sees this normally painfully shy boy grow in confidence and is soon beaming with delight as he accompanies his session teacher on the piano by bashing the drums. By his own admission, Gareth's efforts with drum and tambourine are slightly less than impressive.

Friday 15 April

Get a call from *That Peter Crouch Podcast* asking if I will be a guest on the show with him and Chris Stark. My feeling of being wanted soon evaporates when the story unfolds that they had been trying to get Gareth Southgate and somehow ended up with me! It's all good knockabout stuff, with Pete remembering the time he had a little pop at me after a game at Anfield when one of his goals took a deflection and I asked if he was going to claim it.

He said he was annoyed at the time and, although I couldn't recall the incident, it seemed a fair question to me. Five days later, when the show went out I get a call from Scott Melvin, who was the producer of that particular game, pissing himself laughing as it wasn't me reporting that day but my colleague Guy Havord.

Wednesday 20 April

Chelsea v Arsenal. The pre-match interviews with both managers are reflective of recent results. The Blues have won their last three, including an FA Cup semi-final, so Thomas Tuchel is all smiles, even joking that he recalled Lukaku because we in the media have asked about him so much. The Gunners, on the other hand, have lost their last three and look like blowing their chance of a top four finish and Champions League qualification. Mikel gives monosyllabic answers and I get through about ten questions in the space of two and half minutes. Arsenal win 4-2 and, post-match, Tuchel is in no mood to talk whereas Arteta is effusive in his praise of his young side.

Sunday 24 April

The Merseyside derby is a tense, dour affair for the first hour with Everton frustrating the hosts. Not necessarily pretty but certainly effective. I for one wouldn't criticize them for their approach, when they are not only facing one of the best teams in the world but also fighting for their Premier League lives.

The player that impressed me the most on the day was Anthony Gordon. The twenty-one year old played well, using his guile and pace to have decent claims for one if not two penalties. Post-match he spoke with a maturity way beyond his years, carefully explaining why, although he felt the ref was wrong to book him for diving, he could see why he did. Bright, articulate and willing to engage: a reporter's dream.

Monday 25 April

Lively lunch with Arsène Wenger in his local Italian in north London along with music and football agent, Steve Kutner. Topics include VAR, women's tennis, Premier League domination of the Champions League, Everton's penalty claims, who's going down, Elton John's knowledge of football and a whole lot more. They both know I'm writing a book and we talk about a lot of shared times. The next day, Steve video-calls me, as he is with his long-term client and another old friend of mine, Steve Bould. Bouldy bellows at me, 'I bet you're not going to put in the book that time you were so drunk you fell into my cellar window and I had to pull you out?' He's right, why would I tell anyone about that?

Sunday 1 May

A joyous moment for Arsenal's Rob Holding, who scores his first Premier League goal in an important away victory at West Ham. Alongside him in our post-match interview, goalkeeper Aaron Ramsdale chimes in with, 'It's only taken you six years and a new hairline!' live on TV. Who needs friends like that? But Holding takes it in good heart. David Moyes is spiky in defeat.

Monday 2 May

Get a note from Steve Round, one of Mikel Arteta's assistants. Before opening it, I assume it's going to be about an aspect of our coverage they didn't like. Wrong. He's just had his first hole in one.

Thursday 5 May

Football Writers' Association Dinner at the Landmark Hotel. Liverpool are really impressive as a club tonight, as they lay on a private plane so a delegation, including Footballer of the Year Mo Salah, can attend. This is sandwiched between a Champions League semi-final and playing Tottenham, so an outstanding effort. Salah is gracious and humorous alongside an extremely insightful Ian Rush. Women's Footballer of the Year is Chelsea's Sam Kerr, who is clearly not someone who seeks the media spotlight, but that makes her carefully chosen words even more powerful.

Saturday 7 May

Sit-down interview with Raheem Sterling – and down is the operative word. He's normally upbeat and smiley, but there was just no disguising how much the defeat by Real Madrid in their Champions League semi-final hurt. In the evening, I watch Liverpool versus Tottenham in a Manchester hotel with presenter David Jones and 'The Voice', aka Martin Tyler. We're covering City the next day, so important homework for all three of us. As the goals go in, David writes and re-writes his opening words for the show, The Voice alters his commentary notes and I rethink my questions.

Sunday 8 May

After City trounce Newcastle United 5-0, Jack Grealish and Rodri, in their post-game flash interview, tell us how it was the perfect response to Madrid and how mentally it was so important to get the result. You could feel their relief. Pep Guardiola, on the other hand, goes on the front foot, asking how anyone could have doubted! He ends the interview by declaring City have no fit centre halves but he will play Phil Foden there if they have to. 'Really?' is my astonished response. 'No,' he says with a big grin. Not for the first time, I've been done.

Thursday 12 May

Fifteen years ago, I did a shoot with a young East End boy at a pie-and-mash shop in Dagenham to discuss how, having played twenty-one Premier League games for his beloved West Ham, he was living the dream. Today we sit in exactly the same seats, with Mark Noble having now played precisely 500 games more for the Hammers. The curtain is coming down on a superb one-club career, something he feels will become more of a rarity. His dedication, commitment and professionalism are exemplary.

I remember thinking before we met a decade and a half ago; young lad, could be shy, need to reassure him, etc. When he arrived his first words were, 'All right Shreevesie, you look like you've had plenty of pie 'n' mash.'

Then head west for the North London derby. The atmosphere inside the ground is deafening, and a victorious Harry Kane says it's the best he has experienced there. Credit to Daniel Levy who, I am told, at every single stage of the design and construction would ask what impact any element would have on the acoustics.

Mikel Arteta gives a very limited interview saying if he says what he thinks he would be banned for six months.

Sunday 15 May

At 2-0 up at half-time against Manchester City, it looks like the Hammers are giving their skipper the perfect send-off, as well as conjuring up another twist in the title race. But it ends 2-2 and Noble makes an emotional speech and does a well-deserved lap of honour. To be honest, I wasn't surprised at the lengthy list of former players who wanted to give him a send-off, but I don't think anybody was expecting Prince Albert of Monaco to turn up and give him the royal wave! Turns out he's a friend of a friend.

Tuesday 17 May

Liverpool take it to the last day by beating Southampton 2-1 despite making nine changes. Klopp tells me afterwards 'If we had lost tonight, it would have been on me, not the players.' There is total buy-in from his entire squad.

Friday 20 May

My mood is down at the start of the day, watching the fourth pitch invasion of the week, this time from the previous night's clash at Goodison, where Everton beat Crystal Palace to secure Premier League survival. Thankfully, Patrick Vieira will not face police charges for kicking out at a fan who confronted him, but the FA are investigating. Why, amongst all the jubilation, are there those intent on abusing or even assaulting the opposition? Depressing stuff.

Later, I host a fundraising lunch with Gareth Southgate in aid of Martin House children's hospice. The day takes a decidedly better turn as one lovely person pledges £250,000. Faith in humanity restored.

Sunday 22 May

Déjà vu all over again as Manchester City complete a dramatic comeback from 0-2 down to win 3-2 against Villa and clinch the Premier League title. Impossible not to compare it to the Agüero moment ten years before, from agony to ecstasy, fantastic stuff. Sadly, once again some moron assaults the Villa goalkeeper Robin Olsen during a pitch invasion.

We sweep up plenty of interviews, but perhaps the most touching and poignant is Oleksandr Zinchenko, who weeps as he wraps the Ukrainian flag around the trophy. Fighting back the tears he tells me of his conflicting emotions, which I cannot for one second begin to imagine.

Acknowledgements

There are a number of people who I would like to thank for all their help – without them I would not have been able to publish *Cheers, Geoff!* First and foremost among them is Paul McCarthy. Macca has been a friend for many years and I could not have chosen a better person to chronicle my experiences. His journalistic skills, experience and diligence were crucial in the writing of this book. Plus, he made it a lot of fun. Thank you, Macca.

My agent, Andy Hipkiss, must be credited with the original concept for this book. His initial encouragement and enthusiasm got the ball rolling and he has co-ordinated everything superbly. Well played, Andy. Thanks, as well, are due to my literary agent, James Wills at Watson Little, who showed us what was required to get a successful publishing deal and then negotiated with Macmillan. The team at Macmillan, led by Matthew Cole, have been a joy to work with. Big thanks to Josie Turner, Becca Bryant, Natasha Tulett, Lucy Hale, Stuart Dwyer and Stuart Wilson. For the front cover, thank you to my friend and stylist supreme, Francesca Gray-Walkinshaw, plus photographer Paul Marc Mitchell. Great job, guys. For the audiobook recording, massive thanks to Timothy Brown, the sound engineer, who guided me through with great diligence and care.

Sky have given me an incredible job for over three

decades now and I am truly grateful to them for that and also for the help in writing this book. I have already mentioned countless people in this book who have helped me along the way and I'm sorry if I have left anybody out but there are quite literally too many to mention.

Over the years (decades!) I have been fortunate to have worked with so many excellent producers, directors, talent, APs, travel co-ordinators, fixers, floor managers, make-up artists – the list is endless but so too has been their help.

Lastly, some family credits. Thank you to Jack Shreeves for the transcription work, to Ellie and Lottie Shreeves for the much-needed IT help and, lastly, to Di for having to listen to some of these stories for the ten thousandth time.

Cheers,

Geoff

Picture Credits

All photographs are courtesy of the author apart from:

Page 3 top and page 11 bottom © Sky Sports

Page 5 bottom photo by Manchester City FC via Getty Images

Page 8 bottom photo by Action Images via Reuters/Carl Recine Livepic

Page 9 top © Sharon Latham/Manchester City FC via Getty Images

Page 9 bottom © Matthew Ashton – AMA/Getty Images

Page 10 top © Legends of Football

Page 10 bottom © Matt Kent/WireImage

Page 11 top © Matthew Peters/Manchester United via Getty Images

Page 13 top © Allstar Picture Library Ltd/Alamy Stock Photo

Page 13 bottom © Richard Heathcote – The FA/The FA via Getty Images

Page 15 top photo by David Price/Arsenal FC via Getty Images

Page 15 bottom © Ben A. Pruchnie/Getty Images for Premier League

Page 16 top © Matt McNulty – Manchester City/Manchester City FC via Getty Images